A BASIC COURSE IN DESIGN

...introduction to drawing and painting

by **Ray Prohaska**

North Light

CONTENTS

Page 4 ■ Introduction

6 ■ Geometric Structure of Form

8 ■ First Stage Exercises— Geometric Form

10 ■ Pastel Combined with Linear Design

14 ■ Free-Form Stones and Wood

16 ■ Geometric Free Form

22 ■ Free-Form Exercises— Overlapping Shapes

24 ■ Pen-and-Ink Contour Drawing

28 ■ Contour and Gesture Drawing

32 ■ Mass and Line in Watercolor and Pen Line

36 ■ Watercolor Still Life with Pen

40 ■ Arranging and Interpreting Real Objects

44 ■ The Human Figure

48 ■ Figure Drawing—the Gesture

54 ■ Figure Composition

57 ■ The Monotype or Monoprint

63 ■ Critique of Student Monotype Prints

66 ■ Student Critique All Media

72 ■ Materials and Procedures

74 ■ How to Stretch a Canvas

76 ■ Glossary of Art Terms

INTRODUCTION

Countless books have been written about the theory and practice of the fine arts. Some have become classics of distinguished style and profound philosophical insight. This book does not profess to compete on this level. Instead, I am presenting to the beginner in art a carefully planned crash course, designed to arouse interest in seeing and feeling on the practicing artist's level.

Originally, I designed the course for a two-semester program at Washington and Lee University, where I was artist-in-residence for five years. I offer to a student my experience of over fifty years of professional involvement in the practice of painting, drawing, and illustration.

I have illustrated the following chapters with drawings and paintings done by my students and with occasional works by noted painters, sculptors, and graphic artists. In some cases I have included examples of my own work. This book was designed for the purpose of establishing a rapport between the student-reader and the gifted professional and of further identifying the student's problems by means of examples of successful experiments and accomplishments.

My teaching methods are the result of carefully planned procedures. Heavy emphasis is placed on the understanding of form, spatial concepts, and intuitive response to ideas. It is my belief that stimulating students to adopt disciplined work habits plays an important part in teaching comprehension of visual facts. Progressive exercises in spatial concepts, using various mediums, builds respect for form, preparing the student for more complex investigations into the mysteries of nature. Drawing and painting from the imagination, from still life, and from the human figure become less baffling when approached with some understanding of, and respect for space. The possibilities revealed in the use of various mediums lead the student to a challenging and sophisticated expressiveness.

Definition of Form — a selection from the American College Dictionary.

FORM
Definite shape. External shape or appearance
considered apart from color or material.
Configuration. The shape of a thing or person.
Something that gives or determines shape.
A particular structural condition.
The manner or style of arranging and coordinating
parts for a pleasing or effective result, as in a
literary or musical composition.

To which I add the structure, pattern, organization, or essential nature of anything — to which I further add intellectual, emotional, and physical involvement.

The aspects of *form* with which we shall be concerned are its structural, aesthetic, organic, tactile, and dynamic qualities. We should become deeply involved with, and search out the meaning of, these aspects in order to develop our insight.

Geometric Structure of Form

PAUL CEZANNE believed that for the artist's purpose all the forms in nature could be reduced to geometric shapes — the cube, cone, sphere, and cylinder. I omit the cylinder in these exercises because its shape is compounded from the basic shapes of the sphere and cone. Draw and study these forms in their two-dimensional aspect: square, triangle, and circle. Your aim will be to develop comprehension of form.

I cannot overemphasize the importance of understanding these first exercises thoroughly. I have a twofold purpose in recommending the drawing and arranging of these basic shapes. First of all, it is important to acquire good working habits through discipline and without boredom. You will find that the exercises are a provocative game. You will enjoy the training.

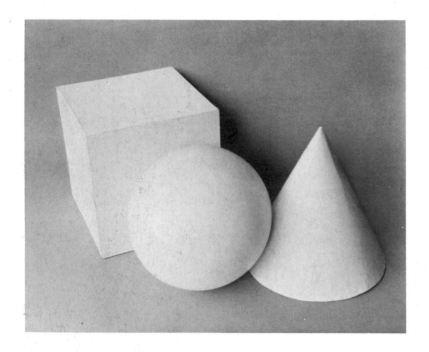

Of all Cézanne's portraits perhaps that of M. Geffroy is the most celebrated . . . The equilibrium so consummately achieved results from the counterpoise of a great number of directions. One has only to imagine what would happen if the books on the shelf behind the sitter's head were upright, like the others, to realize upon what delicate adjustments the solidity of this amazing structure depends. One cannot think of many designs where so complex a balance is so securely held. The mind of the spectator is held in a kind of thrilled suspense by the unsuspected correspondences of all these related elements. One is filled with wonder at an imagination capable of holding in so firm a grasp all these disparate objects, this criss-cross of plastic movements and directions. Perhaps, however, in order to avoid exaggeration, one ought to admit that since Cézanne's day other constructions have been made as complex and as well poised, but this has I think been accomplished at too great a sacrifice of the dictates of sensibility, with too great a denial of vital quality in the forms. Roger Fry: *Cézanne*, Hogarth Press Ltd., London, 1930

First-Stage Exercises — Geometric Form

NOW THAT YOU'VE STUDIED THE PHOTOGRAPH of the cube, cone, and sphere on the preceding page, you can begin to understand the beauty and solidity of these three-dimensional forms.

An appreciation of them will allow you to start benefiting from the exercises before you.

We start by studying these forms in their two-dimensional, or flat, aspects — by learning to arrange them in space with respect for both positive and negative values. By positive, I mean the combined shapes that are organized by you and that reveal a total image regardless of how you group them together. The negative aspect is the white unworked space around these forms, which provides the illusion of space.

After you've absorbed the meaning of the three-dimensional form, concentrate on the flat concept of two dimensions — the square, triangle, and circle. These shapes are equilateral, meaning that the sides are all equal in length and that the diameter of the circle is also equal. Think now of these forms as being made up of straight and curved lines. Practice by drawing these lines until you are confident that you can draw them of equal size and shape without benefit of ruler or compass.

A horizontal arrangement, clearly indicates a feeling of depth with some connotation of drama by the stage-set look.

A well organized grouping with a nice feeling for negative areas — however a bit static in the over-lap color.

In drawing the circle, do one side of it first with a free arm movement. Describe a half-moon arc in the air before you try to draw it. Draw one side in this manner, then the other, joining the two sides to make an approximately perfect circle. Note the proper way to hold the charcoal stick. You will find this difficult at first, but before you know it, you will be drawing nice circles of various sizes. Many of my students concentrate on one shape at a time in their practice. The square is best approached by first drawing an L shape and then joining it with the other side. Once again I stress the importance of drawing the lines of equal length to produce an equilateral shape. The triangle is best drawn by establishing either diagonal side first and then following with the base and finally joining with the other diagonal. I say either side rather than qualifying by saying right or left because right-handed people have a tendency to draw the left side of the shapes first. Left-handed people invariably draw the right sides first.

Free arm movement in drawing is very important, and you should practice this until it becomes an automatic gesture. Developing proper working habits pays big dividends. Draw these shapes on your practice sheet and learn to overlap them until you are very confident; then start the exercises in arrangement. Remember that your working sheet is all-important. It is 18 by 24 inches and is pure white. Start by judiciously drawing one of the shapes on your sheet of paper. Place it so that it has plenty of white negative space around it. This will be your first statement, and you will build your image from this beginning.

Don't be afraid to make a clumsy drawing. If your start is not good, begin again. By doing this you build confidence. Keep your lines clean and consistent in thickness. Apply enough pressure on your charcoal stick to give you a nice line of medium thickness. For these exercises, consistency of line is important to the structure of the forms. Overlap the shapes with forethought so that your inside shapes will be interesting. Once you have gained experience in this area and have established some discipline, everything else will come easier and will be more fun. Remember that in these overlap exercises you are discovering other new and exciting shapes. You are in the process of creating.

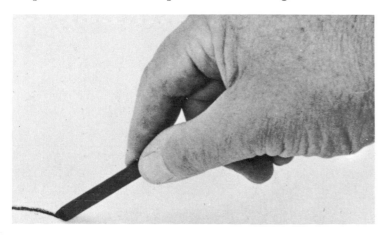

A vertical composition shows the three basic shapes over-lapped with the internal over-lap areas blacked in. The square is placed to one side of the composition to avoid a static look. The black over-lap shapes are strong but detached.

A more complex grouping but a very good arrangement of shapes and a fine selection of over-lap pattern. The black shapes are held together to create a chain reaction image.

Pastel Combined with Linear Design

PASTEL IS AN EFFECTIVE AND ECONOMICAL MEDIUM for this kind of experimentation. When sprayed with fixatif, the drawings retain their brilliance and remain absolutely flat at all times. Pastel has been used by many great artists. You are probably familiar with Degas's ballerinas and his drawings in pastel. Some people call them paintings. Pastel has great lasting quality. The Degas pastels at the Louvre and the Metropolitan Museum appear as fresh as the day they were done. Many other great artists — Manet, Monet, Toulouse-Lautrec, and Odilon Redon, among many others — used pastels. These artists *painted* with pastels, really. They used it in the complete cycle of tone, mass, and line. We, on the other hand, will be using pastel in flat planes, depending on our shapes and images to give us the illusion of depth.

I recommend a box of Grumbacher soft pastels, set no. C, which contains thirty square half-sticks of color.

The scientific use of color is a profound study which has absorbed the lifetimes of many artists and color theorists. At this early point in our experimentation I will not go too deeply into color theory, but will introduce you to the use of the color key wheel, which can be purchased at any art store for $1. This will help you in mixing colors and understanding color harmonies. It is simple to use and is more explicit than any five pages of text I could write to explain it. I do, however, include the color-value chart, which is not included in the color wheel. This chart is reproduced from actual pastel drawings made from the recommended box. The important thing in this chart is value, i.e., the lightness

or darkness of a color. As an example, let's say that you have developed a composition of interesting shapes and overlaps in the geometric space concept area. You have a provocative image with a good organization of black in the overlap areas, and you wish to introduce color without destroying your original black and white concept. It is important to retain your black pattern intact, which means that you must be careful to select color of the right *black and white value* to complete your picture. Dark colors like ultramarine blue, burnt umber, viridian green, violet, and deep cadmium red belong in the dark area on the value scale. These colors can often take the place of black. I am, however, a firm believer in the use of pure black. It does two things to a composition: It strengthens the image, and it gives more meaning to related color.

This discussion on color may seem brief and elementary. However, I have discovered in my years of teaching experience that students acquire a more personal taste in color by developing it in an empirical way. The success of these exercises with students is very convincing to me. Experiencing color stimulation with form enlarges the student's horizon for invention. The student makes his own speculations — there are no rules to this trial-and-error game. As work progresses, the student's personality will come through in his own selection of color. The student may discover that he has a propensity for cool colors with warm accents or that he likes warm or hot colors with cool accents. This is good. It makes for personal statement.

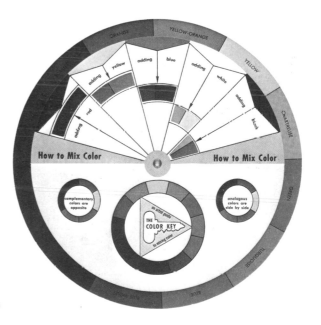

Here the student wanted to retain an unobstructed quality by his use of negative space. The blacks in the center preclude the use of color with too much frontality* such as reds and siennas. He chose instead, cerulean blue, cadmium yellow, and light cobalt violet.

This is not an easy arrangement to handle. The black image cements the three squares and large triangle on the right. The choice of the rectangle in the red squares gives the image a lively relief.

Here color is used to unify the black patterns. Ultramarine blue, cobalt violet and cadmium yellow pale were employed. The blue and violet join forces with the black to extend the pattern without damaging it. Also the yellow in the circle on the left gives depth to the blue triangle.

*the place or position directly before any-thing—as opposed to recessive illusion.

12

Hubert Long, the sculptor, found these pieces of wood on a beach. He arranged them with great respect for space, overlapped them with skill and taste.

Free-form Stones and Wood

NOW WE'RE GOING TO ADD another element to the studies we have made of the organization of geometric forms. This element is the use of free form to give static forms more vitality. You may study the shapes of free form by observing rocks, pebbles, driftwood, microscopic organisms, cloud strata, movements of things in space, and other forms created and conditioned by the forces of nature.

To start your studies in this chapter, I would like you to investigate the shapes of "riverbed rocks" and driftwood. Their simplicity and availability makes these forms preeminent.

A photograph of river bed rocks with a linear diagram showing you what to look for in these shapes and how to see them. Notice too how nature provides an aesthetic balance of "straight lines" and constant change of direction to add structural stability to these shapes. Here you see the simplest and most perfect lesson in drawing such basic shapes.

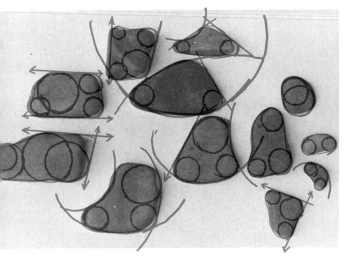

When you start drawing these shapes, your imagination will help you. You will intuitively feel their presence, and the drawings will become a personal statement. Through the experience you gain by investigating the aesthetic implications of these simple elemental forms, you will learn that color and shape exist independently. Our response to color and shape is abstract and basically intuitive. Reason plays a small role in this process.

To illustrate the meaning of "free form," I have photographed an arrangement of rocks found in a riverbed. The infinite variety of shape in these stones makes them worthy of your careful investigation. Understanding their linear structure will play an important role in your experiments in the next two chapters.

1

Geometric Free-form

3

START THESE EXERCISES in geometric and free-form by study-ing the student examples in black and white on page nine. These studies illustrate an infinite variety of very good ar-rangements of these basic shapes. It is prudent to draw in black and white until you have gained confidence in your ability to arrange negative and positive space.

Review your drawings in the geometric area and notice the many tensions created in your arrangements. As you intro-duce the element of free form in your compositions, you will notice a loosening up of these tensions. The fluidity of free-form shapes will make the more rigid geometric shapes more aesthetically acceptable.

To help you get started in this chapter I would like you to study four drawings that I have prepared as a demonstra-tion. A line drawing of two triangles, a square, two circles, and three free-form shapes. You will notice a decidedly more fluid quality in the black patterns created by the overlaps. A black and white photograph of the color composition shown in Fig. 3. This demonstrates the use of color with respect to black and white values. (See color charts.) Add-ing dark-color values in many areas has strengthened the

image considerably. Introducing a dark value of blue in the negative areas dramatizes the image by emphasizing both the staccato white shapes and the warm accent of orange hue.

An all-over pattern of bright cool-color values. This composition clearly demonstrates the prudent use of dark-color values to supplement the use of black. This is clearly seen in the small circle, upper center, where ultramarine blue joins forces with black to complete the spherical image. Again in the butterfly-like free-form shape on the right, cobalt blue is used to complete the rhythm of this free form. The recessive quality of the cool-color values gives prominence and frontality to the warm colors. The sequence of the white shapes is boldly revealed by the use of dark and middle-tone colors. I repeat, this is a cool-color arrangement with one warm-color accent.

A complete reversal in color theme. Here warm and hot color is dominant, while the cool-color (blue) accent plays a double role, that of frontality and that of color accent. To some extent this demonstrates and refutes the theory that cool color is recessive, while warm color projects.

4

This is an arrangement of gay color, predominantly cool, with a prudently placed "hot" triangle. This drawing also cries out for a dominant shape. The student missed several obvious opportunities for tie-ins in the black shapes.

A closely knit image of five geometric and three free-form elements. These are placed with considerable respect for the negative areas. This rather complex image is well contained in line as well as color. This is a good effort.

Here is a composition crying out for one dominant shape. A much larger square could give this arrangement more stability and unity. There is a stinginess about the drawing which cancels out all other values.

A triangle dominates the drawing, which also includes a square and two circles. Three free-form shapes, somewhat statically placed, complete the drawing. This is a tasteful combination of three colors used with restraint.

18

JETTY NO. 2
18 x 22" Tempera on Gesso Panel
Collection Henry Hecht, Washington, D.C.

The use of geometric forms related to reality is clearly illustrated in this painting of mine. The triangle and rectangular shapes are overlapped to create strength and unity. Blue, green and violet establish the mood and presence of the sea without actually showing the water.

LAOCOON • El Greco *(below)*

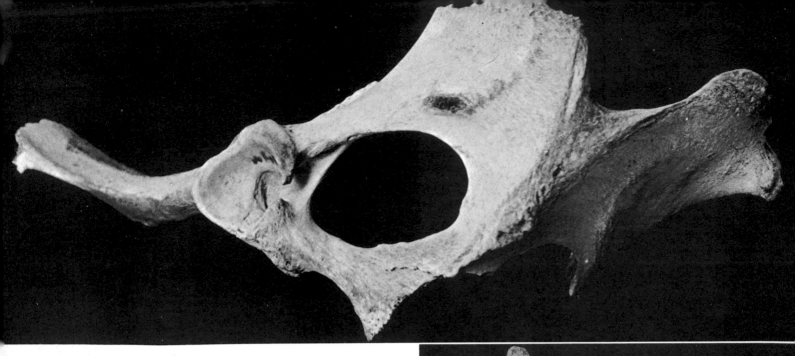

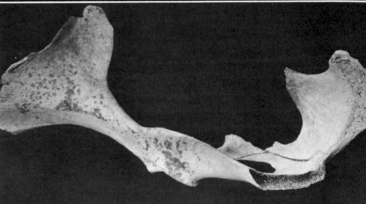

I'VE ALREADY TOUCHED on the meaning of free form. This chapter will carry its exploration further. I've used animal bones to introduce organic shapes.

For the student who wishes to extend his investigations of natural form, I recommend the study of the wonder and complexity of plant life. From the shape and form of a single seed, to the infinite variety of its growth, plant life is structured in an organic way. It grows by a process of repetition of a structural unit — a cell.

Microscropic organisms of living human, plant, and animal life-cell structure challenge our investigation. In their variety and complexity of shape, we can see the potential for artistic application. Artists have studied the cellular structure of many minerals such as steel, iron, copper, brass, uranium, gold, and silver. Scientific investigations into these elements have been illustrated with microscopic color photography. They can be found in the indexes of scientific journals and *Life* magazine.

Accompanying this chapter are photographs of animal bone forms and some reproductions of the work of Henry Moore, the distinguished British sculptor. He has been known to base an entire sculptural concept on the shape and form of an animal bone.

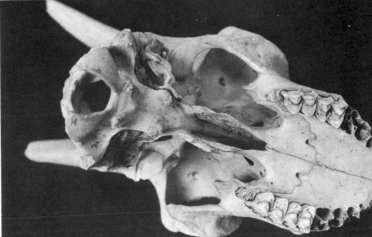

"Notes On Sculpture"

Appreciation of sculpture depends upon the ability to respond to form in three dimensions. That is perhaps why sculpture has been described as the most difficult of all arts; certainly it is more difficult than the arts which involve appreciation of flat forms, shape in only two dimensions. Many more people are "form-blind" than colour-blind. The child learning to see, first distinguishes only two-dimensional shape; it cannot judge distances, depths. Later, for its personal safety and practical needs, it has to develop (partly by means of touch) the ability to judge roughly three-dimensional distances. But having satisfied the requirements of practical necessity, most people go no farther. Though they may attain considerable accuracy in the perception of flat form, they do not make the further intellectual and emotional effort needed to comprehend form in its full spatial existence.

That is what the sculptor must do. He must strive continually to think of, and use, form in its full spatial completeness. He gets the solid shape, as it were, inside his head — he thinks of it, whatever its size, as if he were holding it completely enclosed in the hollow of his hand. He mentally visualizes a complex form from *all round itself*; he knows while he looks at one side what the other side is like; he identifies himself with its centre of gravity, its mass, its weight; he realizes its volume, as the space that the shape displaces in the air. And the sensitive observer of sculpture must also learn to feel shape simply as shape, not as description or reminiscence. He must, for example, perceive an egg as a simple single solid shape, quite apart from its significance as food, or from the literary idea that it will become a bird. And so with solids such as a shell, a nut, a plum, a pear, a tadpole, a mushroom, a mountain peak, a kidney, a carrot, a tree-trunk, a bird, a bud, a lark, a lady bird, a bulrush, a bone.

HENRY MOORE

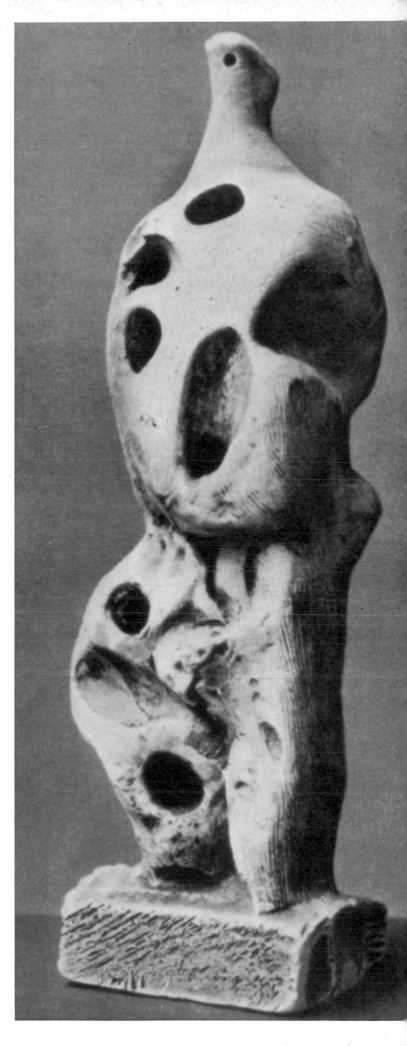

A violet color was used in the negative areas, accented with blue and light yellow ochre to emphasize the white image. They're well arranged shapes in the overlap black patterns. The chain reaction of these shapes was well thought out.

The negative space in this composition is tinted light sienna. The well contained image is developed from shapes motivated by rock forms. Pink and blue are the two dominant colors in the image.

Free-form exercises Overlapping Shapes

Students' color drawings photographed as negative and positive. These examples were selected for the quality of the spatial concepts and the dramatic rhythmic aspects of the compositions. The reversal of the black overlap shapes from black to white in the negative stats reveals a vitality in these shapes not fully appreciated in the positive image. These shapes seem to move like cellular organisms in endless variations.

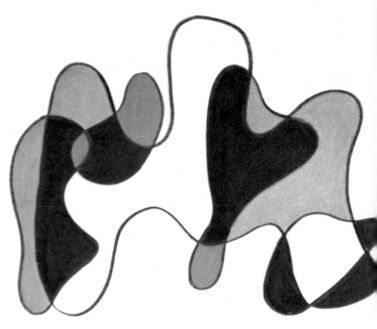

A very well-organized composition of line and mass. The noteworthy thing about this arrangement is the way bright color was used to substitute for black in the overlap patterns.

Black, blue and sienna, a conservative color arrangement that could be greatly improved by joining the two separate images, either with a black shape or with color.

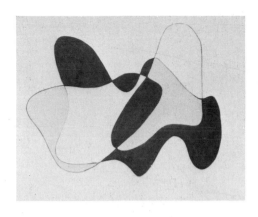

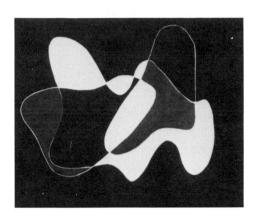

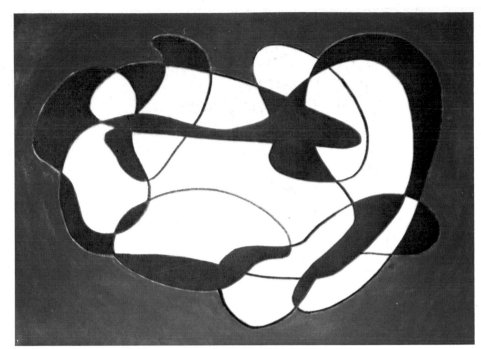

A very simple arrangement of a red ground in the negative area. The image is created in black and white with a strong, emphatic black pattern in the overlap areas. This composition illustrates the prudent use of color to frame a strong pattern. The overlap black shapes glide around the white areas in an uninterrupted way, to frame a strong and provocative image of white against red.

A good logical arrangement of shapes derived from the student's examination of river bed stones. The black overlap shapes are well conceived and frame the central white area, with the red accent contributing to the dramatic concept. Orange and beige are a pleasant complement to the red and black patterns. This is a well thought-out and strong composition.

Pen and Ink Contour Drawing

A CHILD OR A PRIMITIVE begins his drawing with an outline. This naïve line represents truth, regardless of what it describes. The line is beautiful in itself and can be expressive of inner feelings and a strong desire to communicate an idea. The pencil, brush, or pen is an extension of your hand, your mind, and your emotions. To draw a contour you must feel that you have established physical contact with the object you are drawing. As your eye explores the edge of the form, your hand obediently follows this edge and expresses much more than the external contour. Because of its strongly felt presence, the internal structure is also expressed. This awareness makes the difference between a mechanical outline and a contour. Your involvement will manifest a true feeling of what you are drawing by varying degrees of sensitivity in your line. Possessing this sensitivity, the line can express the character of the form you are drawing by the variety of frontality and recessiveness contained in it. Two apples drawn side by side can appear to have different frontality when drawn in contour; herein lies the implication of depth. I am using fruit and vegetables to introduce you to contour drawing because of their availability and their organic and tactile quality and shape. Pick up an apple. Examine its external structure carefully and notice the variety of shape. Cut the apple in two, from the stem down, and examine its internal structure.

I am anticipating your first questions before you start drawing. How do you look at the model? What particular quality should you investigate? Where is it the roundest? Why does it appear flat on some sides? Why does it seem to lean? How does the internal structure affect my drawing? These and many other questions will be partially answered by studying the accompanying diagrams of apples, mushrooms, and green peppers.

Note the different way the hand is held in this exercise: My hand is well off the paper, allowing me complete freedom in developing a line. This way of holding the pen may feel awkward at first because of the lifelong habit of writing with the hand resting on the surface. A little practice will correct this. Use fresh fruit for your models. Start with a few pieces, just enough for one day's drawing. A couple of apples, two green peppers, a pear, and a few mushrooms will start you off. The fruit and vegetables will keep their shape for several days, especially if you refrigerate them at night.

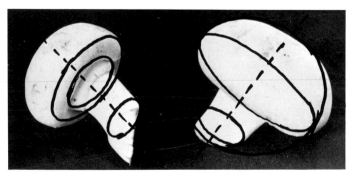

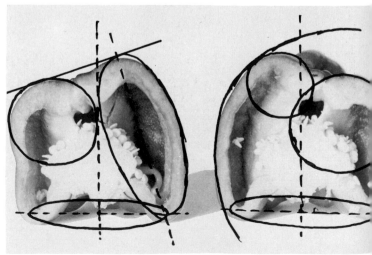

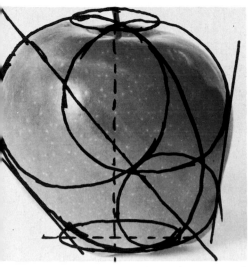 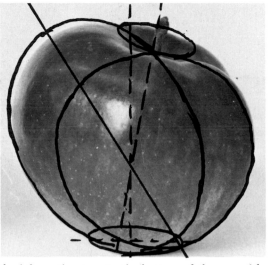 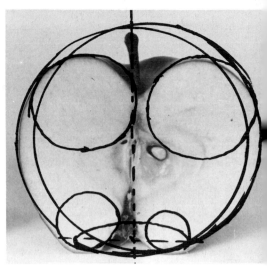

Although the center of the fruit is established from the stem to the bottom of the core (the straight dotted vertical line), the fruit nevertheless looks as if it were leaning to the left. The diagram indicates the presence of an oval with its axis to the left. Straight lines at each side of the fruit give it a special character. Nature (growth) has conditioned this apple very much as nature (force of water) conditions the stones of a river bottom. Be aware of the same spherical and straight lines of force in the fruit that you see in stones and driftwood. Study the diagrams; they will help you to "see" the fruit and structural forms so that you can draw its contour and gesture with understanding.

CONTOUR DRAWING

Set up the fruit or vegetables you want to draw directly in front of you. Before you start drawing, pick up the pieces and examine them from all sides, top and bottom. Cut an apple in two with a sharp knife from the stem down. Do the same with the pepper and the mushroom or pear. Study the internal structure of these models and notice how more complex the internal structure of the pepper is, what interesting possibilities it has for drawing. Notice the relationship between the internal and the external structure. Keep both in mind when you draw the contour.

With your models directly in front of you, start looking very hard at the outer edge of the form and let your eye roam freely around the various contours. Trace the path of the contour with your index finger until you are familiar with every bump and depression. Now, dip your pen in the ink and hold the pen over the area where you wish to start your drawing. Look at the model and not your paper. Because you have peripheral vision you will be able to partially see your paper, even though you are concentrating on the model. Let your mind and eye follow the outer edge of the form, and your hand will respond to this visual investigation. It will be difficult at first, and you will make many trial drawings before you acquire the feel of drawing. If you find that your hand and pen "get lost" and fall off the contour, look at your paper and relocate at the point where your drawing was most convincing. Don't be concerned about mistakes — they will be interesting to see later. Many of the great masterpieces of drawing reveal the artist's search of his form with various trial runs in line still visible on the finished drawing.

MATERIAL RECOMMENDED FOR CONTOUR DRAWING

A bottle of India ink (Higgins) or (Pellican) waterproof. A plain pen holder and a box of pen points, No. 513 bowl point, made by Hunt Globe Co. This is an ordinary writing pen point and should be available at any school supply or stationery store. The bowl point of this pen point allows you complete freedom of line. It will not stick into the paper as some drawing nibs will do. Another important reason for using this pen with India ink is the quality of line that is possible with this combination. A fountain pen or felt pen is not recommended because they produce a line of one thickness of mechanical measure. This rigid limitation precludes any possibility of creating lines with sensitivity.

The next items on the materials list are bond paper, pad size 14 by 17 inches, 16-pound weight, and several pieces of clean rag. When you are working with India ink, you must wipe the pen point occasionally to allow free flow of ink; otherwise the ink will gum up at the point and your lines will blot.

Notice in the student's trial contour drawings that the preoccupation is with sensitivity of line and not pictorial quality.
I will repeat what I have already mentioned in this chapter,
that your lines, possessing sensitivity, can express the character of the form you are drawing by the variety of frontality
and recessiveness contained in them. A very good measure
of this dimension can be seen on page 27. Notice this quality
of depth by variety of line shown in the excellent drawing
of mushrooms.

The experience you gain in contour drawing from fruit and
vegetables will prove to be a valuable asset in your involvement with figure drawing. In a later chapter devoted to
figure drawing we will study contour drawing from the
more complex human form. We will also study gesture.
What the model is doing, regardless of the action, is gestured
— it can be completely relaxed and have gesture. Even our
simple form, the apple, has gesture; everything has gesture.

Contour and Gesture Drawing

THE CRUSHED OR CRUMPLED PAPER MODEL is a simple device which you make yourself. Take a piece of bond paper from your 14 by 17 inch pad. Hold the center of the long edges in each hand and give the paper a vigorous twist and at the same time crushing it. This will form a sculptured mass containing interesting surface relationships, tensions, hills, valleys, tunnels and spherical rhythms. A little experimenting will teach you how to attain much variety of form with the paper.

These willing if somewhat complicated models can be turned and twisted to provide you with a variety of views. Black paper can also be used.

You might find drawing these forms baffling at first, because of their apparent complexity. For this reason I recommend that you start drawing the outer edge of the form. How to evaluate these shapes is clearly demonstrated with diagrammatic drawings made from photographs of the actual models. These diagrams are intended to help you to "see" and "look" at the model but they should in no way influence the quality of contour line that you use to express the form.

A black paper form with a strong jagged edge on the right side reveals six changes of direction in line. Notice the effect of this jagged shape on the negative "shaded" area. The internal contours all come to a peak at the center of the form.

This dramatizes the internal contours by the way the little lady bug strolls over the surface to describe the hills and valleys.

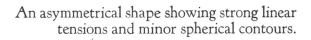

An asymmetrical shape showing strong linear tensions and minor spherical contours.

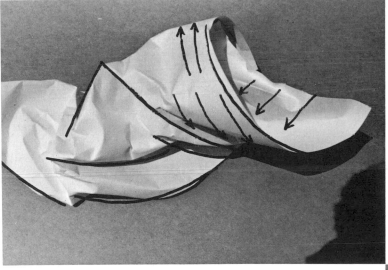

A strong twisted shape revealing many spherical rhythms, and an interesting gesture.

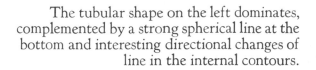

The tubular shape on the left dominates, complemented by a strong spherical line at the bottom and interesting directional changes of line in the internal contours.

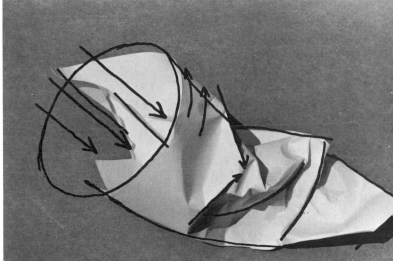

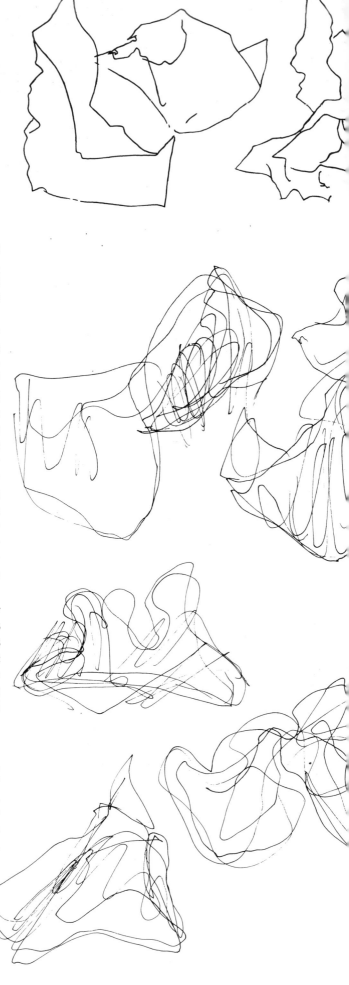

CONTOUR DRAWING —

Set up the model in front of you and start drawing by letting your mind and eyes follow the outer edge of the form. If your concentration is good your hand should obey these impulses. Follow the example of the student drawings opposite. Place several drawings on one page, with respect for space. Try for subtle variety of line to create the illusion of depth. Draw the models from many different angles. You'll find each angle a new experience.

GESTURE OF CRUSHED PAPER

All animate as well as inanimate objects have gesture. The implication of gesture in these paper sculptures is evident. The gesture of these shapes should be done with speed and fluidity of line, using almost split second comprehension to express only the flash aspect of the model.

After you have drawn the "edge" of the crushed paper contour many times, you are ready to enlarge your experience by including the more complex internal shapes in your drawings. Try several different ways of starting the drawings of the complete form. Start with the center of the crushed paper and work out to the edge of the form. This can be difficult unless you fully understand the character of the twist or crumple. Follow the direction of the folds, the hills and valleys; they will inevitably lead your pen to the outer edge. Remember to look at your model and not at your drawing. Trust your intuition, if you get lost re-locate at the point where your pen began to wander off the track. Leave your mistakes, forget them and continue drawing with confidence. Feel the quality of your line. Every change of direction or a new found fold can result in a change of sensitivity in your line. This sensitivity contributes to the recessiveness and frontality of the line, resulting in the illusion of depth.

The crumpled paper contains many forces, tensions and organized planes, working together and in opposition. Curves unite with stratified vertical, diagonal and horizontal shapes to point up the character of the crumple and its ultimate mass. In the vitality and organization of these planes you can see one of Nature's lessons; for these are the same forces that have shaped the physical manifestations of the earth and moon, from the mountain ranges to the tundra.

Note the group of rapid flash gesture drawings on this page. Make your own gesture drawings filling many pages. I repeat, don't be concerned with pictorial quality, allow your vision, mind and pen to orchestrate in full rhythm. These exercises from crushed paper models will be a rewarding experience in your investigation of the human figure as well as the many other interesting areas from which you learn.

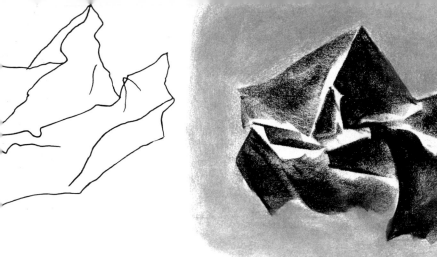

MODELED DRAWINGS IN PASTEL AND PEN AND INK

The reason for these exercises in modeled drawing is to give the student some tactile experience in form; to feel the weight, the bulk and mass of the object. Think of the modeled image as a sculptural form and conceive it from the inside, or the core. If you were working in a sculptor's studio you would start all your concepts of form with the core or the sculptor's armature. You would naturally build all other shapes and forms from this central beginning.

Study the center drawings.

They were rendered with two pastels from your color box: black and gray. There are two grays in the pastel selection — one is a cold bluish gray and the other is a warm tone. Either is good for this exercise. I recommend the pastel because it is always ready and a fast medium for this kind of effort. Use the side of your chalks and, start your mass drawings from the center and work out to the edge. The pastel will help you to visualize the crisp quality of the shapes in the paper form.

The first was made from black construction paper.

The next demonstrates the way to approach the bulk drawing by starting in the center of the form.

Finally, there's the pen and ink rendering using the "birdsnest" idea of cross hatched lines to create the illusion of bulk. Quoting from *The Natural Way to Draw* by the late Kimon Nicolaïdes, the famed instructor and artist from the Art Students League, "Start in the center of the form and work out toward all the surfaces."

In the next chapter we will pursue a closely related idea, using water color and pen line to explore the potential of line and mass with abstract images.

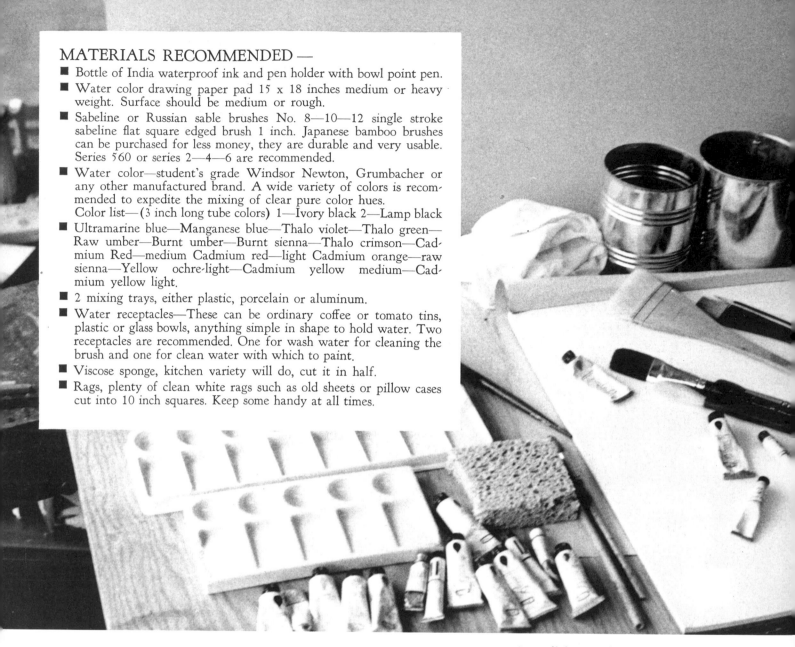

MATERIALS RECOMMENDED —

- Bottle of India waterproof ink and pen holder with bowl point pen.
- Water color drawing paper pad 15 x 18 inches medium or heavy weight. Surface should be medium or rough.
- Sabeline or Russian sable brushes No. 8—10—12 single stroke sabeline flat square edged brush 1 inch. Japanese bamboo brushes can be purchased for less money, they are durable and very usable. Series 560 or series 2—4—6 are recommended.
- Water color—student's grade Windsor Newton, Grumbacher or any other manufactured brand. A wide variety of colors is recommended to expedite the mixing of clear pure color hues.
  Color list— (3 inch long tube colors) 1—Ivory black 2—Lamp black
- Ultramarine blue—Manganese blue—Thalo violet—Thalo green— Raw umber—Burnt umber—Burnt sienna—Thalo crimson—Cadmium Red—medium Cadmium red—light Cadmium orange—raw sienna—Yellow ochre-light—Cadmium yellow medium—Cadmium yellow light.
- 2 mixing trays, either plastic, porcelain or aluminum.
- Water receptacles—These can be ordinary coffee or tomato tins, plastic or glass bowls, anything simple in shape to hold water. Two receptacles are recommended. One for wash water for cleaning the brush and one for clean water with which to paint.
- Viscose sponge, kitchen variety will do, cut it in half.
- Rags, plenty of clean white rags such as old sheets or pillow cases cut into 10 inch squares. Keep some handy at all times.

Mass and Line in Watercolor and Pen Line

IN THIS CHAPTER you will be working with a mixed media. This means that you'll use more than one medium to create the art. Use water color to express the shapes and arrangements of abstract patterns to form the mass of the image. On top of this mass you will impose a fluidly conceived line. This line is juxtaposed on your mass color patterns to produce challenging color rhythms in line and mass. The linear patterns are conceived independently of the mass patterns to oppose the mass and at the same time to establish unity. This line explores the color field with a nervous intensity, inducing a counter-rhythmic force. These calligraphic overtones, free and independent as they are of the mass, produce kinetic forces in the composition. I often use a musical analogy to explain this force to my students by comparing it to a counter melody in a musical composition.

In this area you are actually starting to create paintings with ideas, form and color. These same exercises are valuable as rehearsals for future efforts in painting or graphics media.

Prismatic color which is formed by the refraction of light through a transparent prism is brilliantly pure. Water color, when used transparently without white pigment, is the

BURNING OF THE HOUSES OF PARLIAMENT — 1834 J. M. W. Turner

purest medium next to prismatic color. Washes are clear, crisp and brilliant. A wash of color may be applied to the paper and allowed to dry thoroughly before you apply another color over it. You can obtain beautiful color hues in this manner. For example: yellow and red overlapped over blue will create various hues of violet, purple and green. This overlapping of color is a process of discovery very much like the experience you have had in geometric and free form drawing where you were discovering interesting new shapes. Here you'll discover exciting new colors. There are many other ways of painting in watercolor. One very popular and effective way of applying water color is called, "wet into wet," technique where colors are applied with plenty of water and allowed to blend into each other spontaneously. J. M. W. Turner, the great English painter, used fluid water color washes to paint his extraordinary pictures. *The Burning of the Houses of Parliament* from his sketchbook is a brilliant example.

In contrast there is John Marin's water color of a New York scene, powerfully expressed with moving shapes of brilliant color made up of flat and modeled color hues.

RED SUN BROOKLYN BRIDGE — 1922 John Marin

STARTING TO PAINT

Prepare your palette for painting by squeezing a generous amount of color out of each tube into the wells of the palettes. Start with the darkest colors on the left and move to the lighter on the right. Ultramarine blue—manganese blue, thalo violet, thalo green, raw umber, burnt umber, burnt sienna, Raw sienna, Yellow ochre, Cadmium yellow, medium Cadmium yellow light. (Don't use black for this exercise.)

Fill your two water receptacles with cool water and have sponges and rags handy. Prepare the water color paper by wetting the surface with a sponge. Rinse out the sponge until there is just enough water in it to wet the paper. This avoids any chance of the paper resisting the washes.

I suggest this because, in paper manufacture, chemicals or machines often leave a residue of greasy substance on the surface. Even though this is slight, it can still damage your washes.

You will learn to use your color by experience. However, the color sketches done by my students will help you to form some decisions of your own.

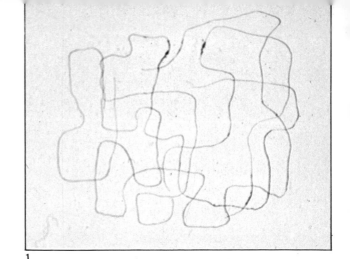

1

2

Color is grouped into two areas, cold and dark colors on the left, warm and light colors on the right. In the dark area left there's violet on top, a sienna brown and dark blue. The center of the right top is cadmium red, light cadmium yellow and deep and pale warm green made with small amount of thalo green with cadmium yellow, light.

Notice that the colors are painted loosely using plenty of water and allowing a certain amount of bleeding on the edges. Let the ragged edges come naturally. Allow the brush freedom to form them casually. Leave whatever happens alone, don't work into the patterns. A spontaneous shape is better than an overworked one. Think of the "big idea" at hand, your space concept, the color harmony and the total image. Remember that on top of this color statement there'll be a line which will have its own authority.

1. The line has been drawn without lifting the pen from the paper.

2. Demonstrating the independent quality of the line. Notice that no part of the color image has been defined by this line.

3. A forceful double image exerting a strong quality to the arrangement.

4. A rather static use of color shapes, and the linear pattern is too square.

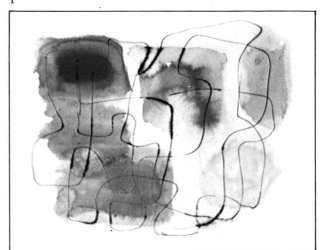

3

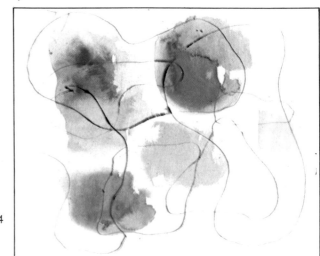

4

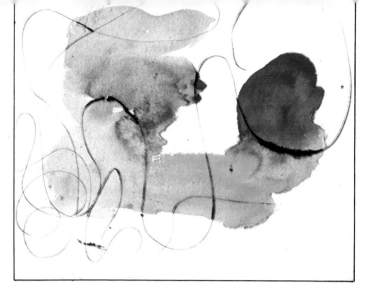

5. This is a good example of mass and line contributing to the unity of the whole.

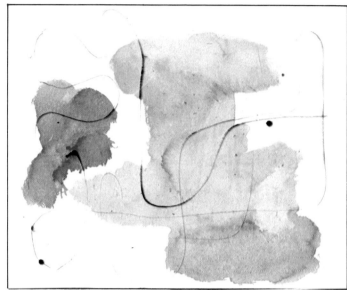

6. The lightness of the colors allows the line to move freely throughout the composition. In crossing over the yellow and blue shapes, the line contributes a feeling of depth.

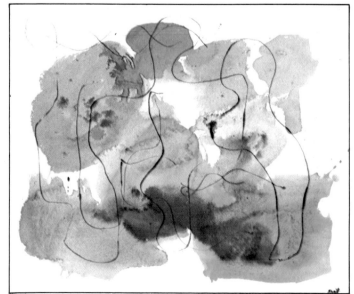

7. This arrangement is an excellent example of how you can use wet into wet color effectively. The line, although forcefully independent, does not contribute much to the whole.

8. Notice the soft edge at the bottom of the crimson shape. This was accidentally caused by a wet spot in the paper. Two happy little spots of warm yellow and one light blue spot are tastefully placed to complement the large image. I would prefer his linear work if it were more intuitive and less formal.

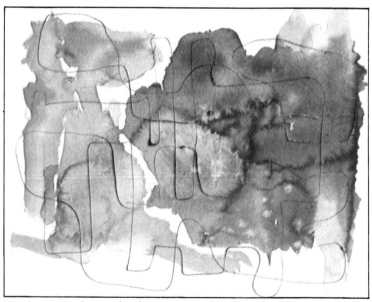

9. A very good example of wet into wet blending of color producing a kaleidoscopic effect. The line is a little too architectural and too intellectualized. A line that moved with abandon throughout this composition would have improved it.

35

The wax flowers, vase and drapery are analyzed in a diagramatic drawing.

Watercolor Still Life with Pen

examples of students' work ——➤

IN THE PREVIOUS CHAPTER we were concerned with mass and line, using abstract elements of color combined with independent line. We will apply the same technique using watercolor and pen line, except that we will be interpreting reality. In our school studio we used artificial flowers because they were always available. The idea of using paper or wax flowers is not new. Paul Cézanne did some remarkable paintings from them. Naturally we would prefer to use fresh flowers, so use them if they are available.

Assuming that you'll be using fresh flowers, I'd like you to select a wide variety of shapes and colors. Select a vase that is very simple in shape; color isn't important. A piece of material can be draped under the vase to suggest the texture of folds. The presence of these flowers does not imply that we are about to start imitating nature by painting the model in a realistic fashion. On the contrary, we'll be concerned only with personal interpretation of the objects. You'll get color and shape responses from the model which you should translate to your paper in color and shape of selective order. Recreate not only what you see in the flowers, but what you feel about them. As an example, this freedom to re-create the reality may result in a desire to translate the image of a red rose into a blue pattern that will be a more desirable color in that place on your composition.

In the previous chapter mass was distinguished by the quality of shape, color spontaneity and the environment of the whole. Line, although conceived independently of the mass, nevertheless contributed to the character of the abstract image.

In this chapter the mass is an interpretation of reality. Here realistic statements of fact are recreated with strong use of color and shape to echo the reality in a very personal and ambiguous way.

color interpretation from the model.   quality of the line   both the mass and line

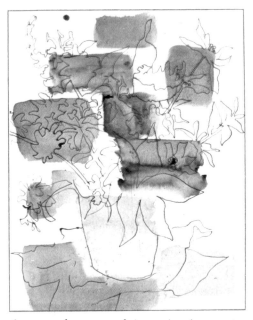

A very pleasant and inventive interpretation of "cubed" high key color with very well considered delineation. It shows nice respect for spatial values.

Fluid and high key color working extremely well with a confident line that searches out the floral shapes with authority.

The two dark red flower shapes in this composition seem to give depth and meaning to the pale blue and yellow shapes. The pink and orange in the cloth are a happy combination.

The student who did this used vertical rectangles to suggest his flower shapes. The line drawing is confidently done and moves out of the rigid vertical shapes to complete a very provocative composition.

Matisse

Cezanne

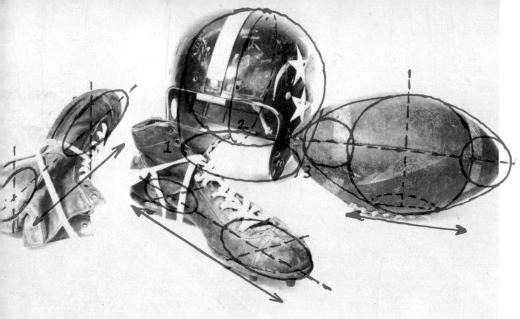

Arranging and Interpreting
Real Objects

THE USE OF FOOTBALL GEAR in the still-life was circumstantial. I had been teaching in a men's college; and several of my students were on the football team, hence, the handy stuff. The helmet and ball are basic shapes and the shoes present an interesting drawing problem.

So far our experience with charcoal line and pastel has been limited to drawing and coloring the basic form exercises. The problems were abstract. We were not interpreting any natural forms in a realistic way. Our basic forms were influenced by the shapes and structure of river-bed rocks and driftwood from the sea.

My reason for switching you back to charcoal line and pastel at this point is that I think that, by using this simple technique, you'll be more inclined to concentrate on pattern and color balance and less on technique and mood. I also believe that it's a good idea to experiment with various mediums in many areas. I'd also like to recommend sketching outdoors with pastel and charcoal, concentrating on interesting fragments of nature that offer possibilities for studying natural forms. Old gear around boats, boat yards, harbors and docks, can be exciting to draw and a challenging potential for interpretation in line and color.

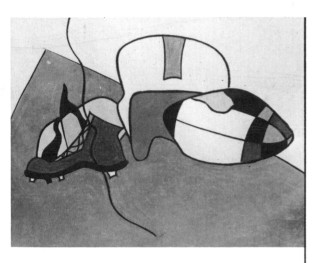

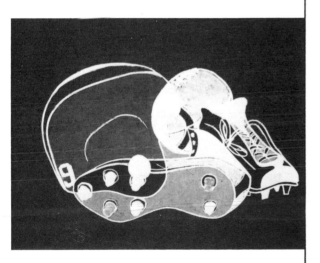

Now we're going to explore the possibilities of drawing, arranging and interpreting real objects. Set up your own still life by selecting shapes that are available to you. For example, you may substitute an old fashioned tea kettle or a colander for the helmet. This will give you the massive round form. A coffee pot on its side, a pair of old shoes, sneakers, galoshes or almost anything that's close at hand. Whatever you choose to interpret will create the atmosphere for investigation. Whenever possible I would prefer the student to work from life or still life. However, there is something to be learned by drawing from the photograph of the models in this chapter.

The helmet is composed of a sphere, and it rests on three points described by the oval under the sphere. The center white line is described by a narrowed oval. The football is composed of a small circle at each end joined by the larger circle in the center. Notice how it rests on a small area described by the dotted oval at the bottom. The shoe on the left, on its side, rests on two small ovals—the arrow points the direction of the shoe in the composition. The other shoe, standing, rests on two small ovals. Being aware of these simple facts will be a great help in drawing these shapes.

The three examples of students' work on the left illustrate dramatically why it is important to have the same regard for the negative space around the objects as you have for the positive image. Notice the negative reverse images. See how beautifully the black areas compose with the white and gray. To get a fresh look at your own drawing or painting, hold it up to a mirror. This often exposes faults and virtues you won't otherwise see.

Overlapping these realistic shapes can provide the same sense of discovery that we experienced in the basic exercises. Many works of Picasso and Braque reveal brilliant use of overlapped realistic shapes to heighten pictorial and visual impact.

The examples of my students' work on the next page were among the best done. Many of them were later developed into successful paintings.

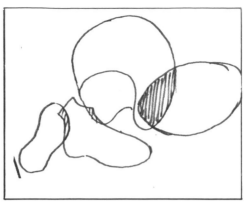
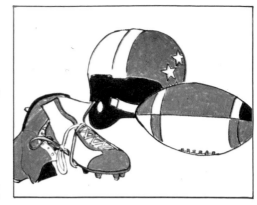

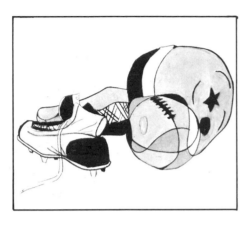
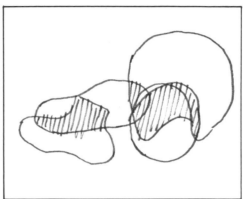
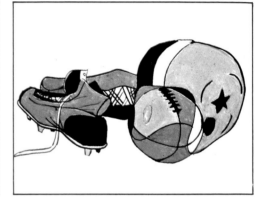

Braque

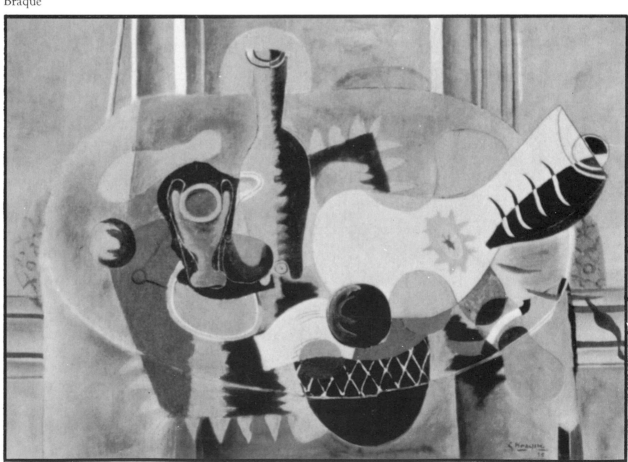

42

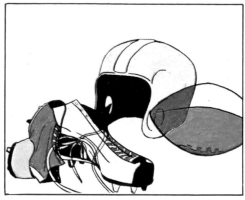

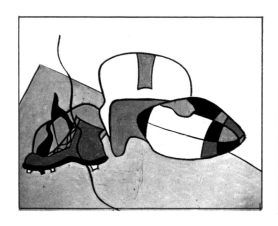

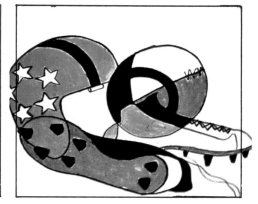

Picasso

43

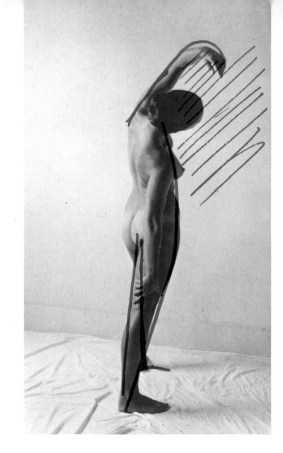

The Human Figure

IN THIS CHAPTER we will be concerned with the beginning of figure drawing. You might wonder why I have taken so long to bring you up to this very important area. My reason is that we have been learning much about form and space, and through basic exercises in these various areas we have gained some knowledge of the visual language. We have learned to respect the space in which we work in the picture plane. We are also more familiar with the shapes of things, and the forces that condition these shapes. The divine forms of man and woman are the most complex of all natural shapes. To try to see the human figure clearly without knowledge of form and space is a baffling experience. To know how and where to start a drawing from the human figure requires that you learn how to *see,* how to *look at,* and how to *feel* the presence of the model. To do this with success, you must consider all aspects of form.

Every pose that the model assumes, whether it is active or passive, contains rhythmic forces. To be able to draw these gestures quickly you must make a mental evaluation of the pose before you decide how to render it. With a good knowledge of forces, tensions and rhythms you can make this decision with authority. You draw the significant gesture or contour that describes exactly what the model is doing. You nail it down quickly.

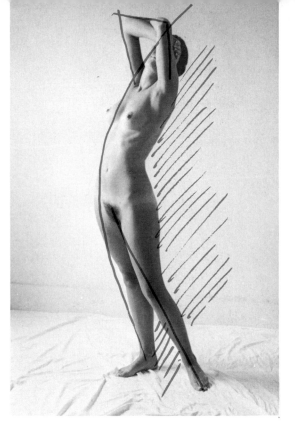

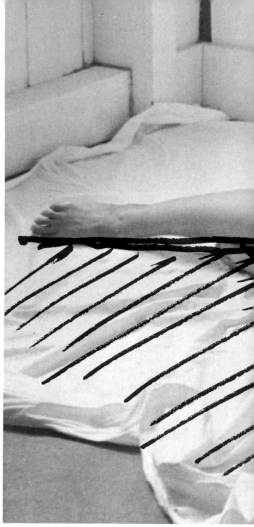
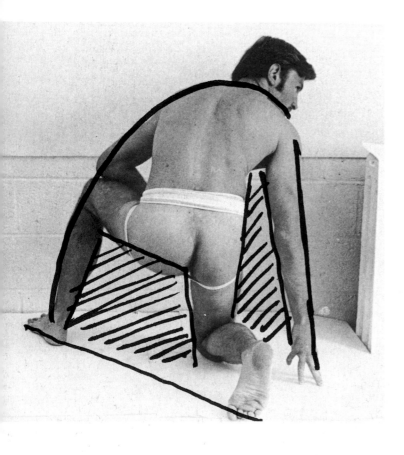

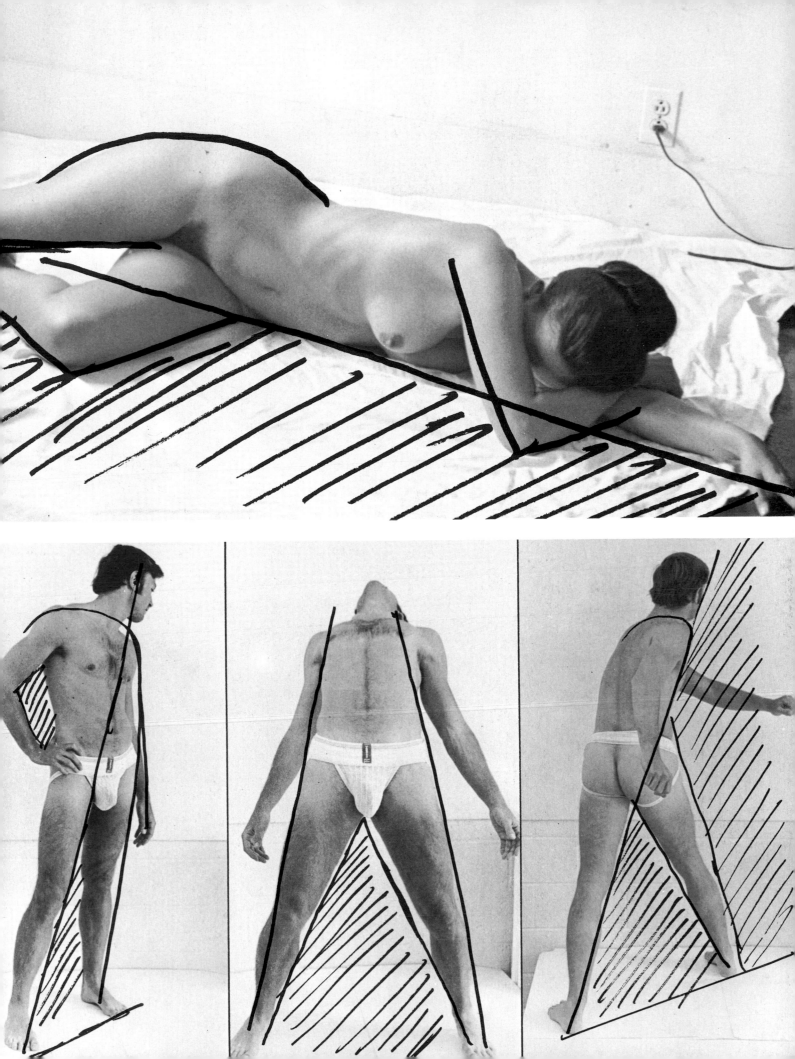

Figure Drawing — the Gesture

THE DEFINITION OF GESTURE—a mode of action, carriage, or posture; a motion of the body or limbs intended to express an idea or a passion, or to enforce or emphasize an argument, assertion, or opinion. In simpler terms it means "what a person is doing."

Because I am an ardent surf fisherman I naturally do a lot of walking on the beach. I have often recognized an old friend, long before I could see his face, by the way he was casting and by his posture as he stood in the water. The human gesture is as personal as the fingerprint. The way a man walks, bends, runs, moves his arms and his legs, jumps, or scratches his head, reads a newspaper or just sits quietly can clearly identify him.

Gesture is not limited to humans or animals. Inanimate objects also have gesture. We see an example of this in the way Cezanne painted apples. Each fruit has its own character in color and gesture; no two of Cezanne's apples are alike. Look at things around you; they all show a gesture, a newspaper lying on the floor can exhibit an emphatic gesture, so can a kettle, a hat on a rack, a curtain, a cloud, a tree, a branch, a stalk of corn, or a chair.

To draw gesture you can use lithograph crayon, pencil, vine or pressed charcoal, pen and ink, brush and ink or brush and paint. In our school-studio we used pressed charcoal, the same No. 2 grade that you used for the basic drawing exercises. By drawing with the side of the charcoal stick, you can achieve a broadly delineated stroke of varied densities. This helps you to make a firm statement of your response to the model. In this same way you can describe the bulk and mass of the figure. Search out the form with free flowing strokes; work over the entire form using a circular motion to express the roundness. Start with the core — the center of the form — and work out to the edge.

You can describe the linear aspects of gesture with the same charcoal stick. By holding the stick about two inches from the point, you will be able to see your lines developing unobstructed by your fingers or hand.

The pen line is a very effective way to express gesture. Various illusions of depth can be achieved by searching out the form with a fluid, insistent line. Pay close attention to the volume, mass and space around the figure. Walk around the model so that you can understand the gesture from all sides. Study the forces that are contained in the pose. Identify with the model by holding the pose yourself. Feeling the tensions will help you decide your visual treatment of the gesture.

The materials that you will be using in gesture drawing are already familiar to you: pressed charcoal, india ink, pen and a pad of bond paper 15x18 inches.

Pose the model directly in front of you about eight to ten feet away. Place your bond pad on a drawing board so that any horizontal or vertical lines in the room "square" with the four sides of your paper; this will help your recognition of gesture.

Prohaska

48

1   2   3

Concentrate on what the model is doing; remember, gesture is not necessarily an *action*. A model sitting quietly has gesture. I repeat, walk around the model; study every aspect of her gesture. Identify with the model, and put yourself in her pose so that you feel the tensions.

Look at the model as you draw, not at your paper. Make swift passes with your pen or charcoal; draw only the essential lines that express briefly what you see and feel. If you suspect you've lost your line, that it has fallen off the form, re-locate. Start again at the point where the line left the figure. Leave your mistakes, for you will learn from them later.

You will learn more about gesture drawing as I take you through the procedure of analyzing my students' drawings. Each critique will contain information with a direct bearing on that particular effort.

Illustrations 1-2-3 are one minute drawings done with the flat side of the charcoal stick. Make as many of these brief drawings as the time will allow; by changing your position you will have a fresh look at the gesture from all sides of the model. After you have worked for about an hour, switch to pen and ink. Drawings 4-5-6 pen and ink gesture were done with much fluidity of line. The line seems to roam over the entire form in a restless way, each pass contributing to the visual impact of the whole. Drawings 7-8-9 are an extended effort in gesture, done with more desire to express bulk in mass line drawing. Here the "birds nest" conglomerate line is used very much like soft wire is used for sculpture concepts. No. 7, a sitting pose where the spiral line contributes to the depth illusion in the model's foreshortened leg. The cross hatched spherical mass of the head contains this shape in a tone. No. 8 echoes this idea by expressing the entire form. No. 9, aside from the student's preoccupation with a vital part of the anatomy, the gesture here is quite good.

Your experience with comprehension of form, your work with contour drawings of fruit, vegetables, and crushed paper, and your practice in gesture drawing have prepared you for this chapter. Contour drawing of the human figure can be difficult and baffling. Your study of basic forms should allow you to approach this problem with confidence, and to understand that the many complexities of the human form make up one simple structural unit.

You can learn a great deal by observing student examples and professional drawings and by close attention to my explanation of procedure. However, you'll learn even more from actual experience and practice in the drawing of the human form.

Assuming that you are now prepared for this phase of contour drawing, I will analyze the student drawings to complete this chapter.

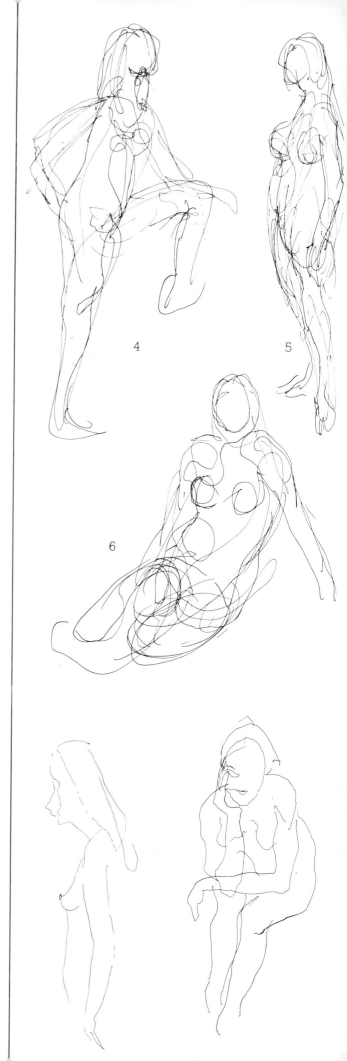

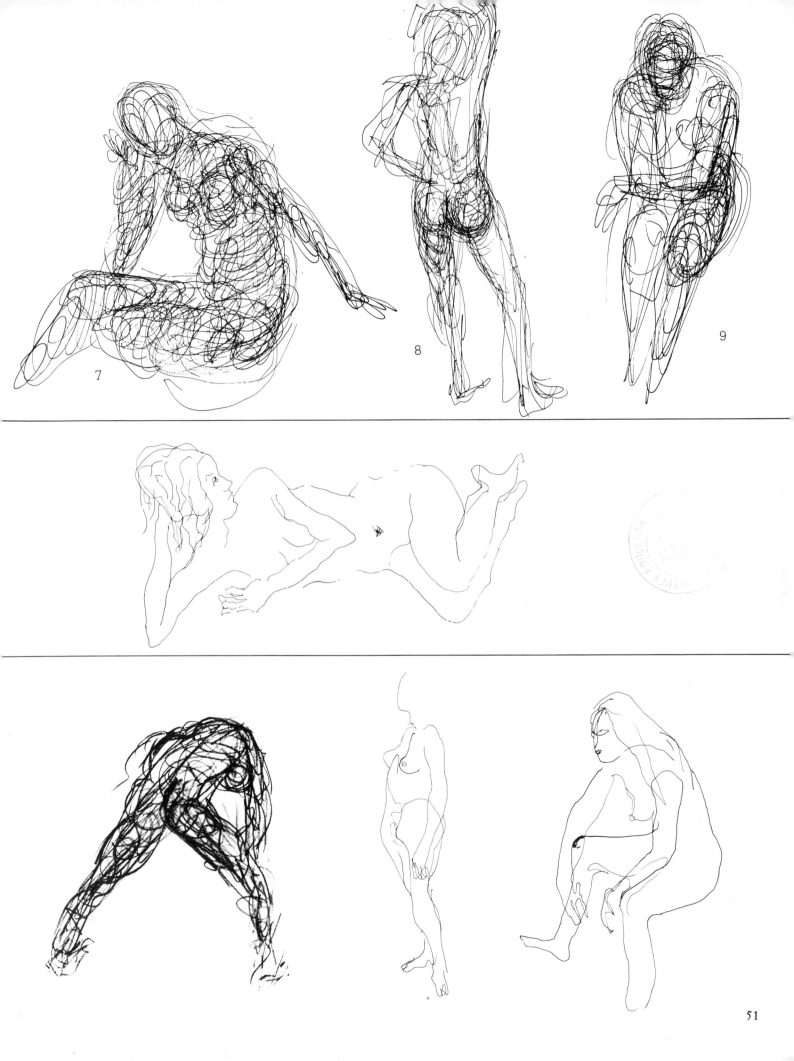

7

8

9

There seems to be an urgency in this drawing that was probably motivated by the difficulty of the pose. The student expressed the tension shown in this gesture well with swift, sure strokes of his charcoal.

A pose such as this can rarely be held for more than a minute, this accounts for the sense of urgency shown in the drawing. The gesture is well expressed through economy of effort. This drawing shows experience and concentration.

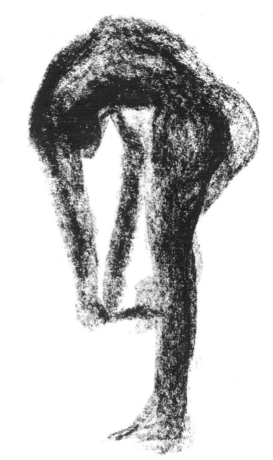

Using the side of the charcoal, the student contained this gesture well in simple statements rendered with authority.

This honest and direct drawing was quickly rendered with the side of the charcoal. The student displays confidence and understanding.

◄ This excellent drawing shows swift and skillful use of the charcoal and respect for tactile form.

This boxer-like gesture done with the dulled point of the charcoal stick contains too much preoccupation with surface rendering to be a good gesture drawing.

THE DESCENT FROM THE CROSS • Van Der Weyden

Figure Composition

WE WILL BE CONCERNED NOW with figure composition, using pressed charcoal and color pastel. Draw each figure directly from the model with a strong black charcoal line. Make the drawing brief and describe the gesture in the simplest terms. The model will hold each pose for five minutes. You have a choice of drawing each pose first and making the arrangement later, or you can tackle the more challenging problem by drawing and arranging at the same time. The latter is much more difficult and requires forethought. Each figure drawn must complement the other by the gesture, black over-lap patterns, color and spatial relationships. Either way, you must accept or reject the poses offered by the model on the basis of their potential value to the whole structure.

The student chose to repeat sitting and squatting poses to maintain the force of his vertical figure.

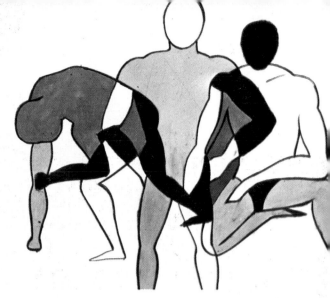

The most impressive statement in this composition is made by the blue, violet and black overlap patterns running across the image.

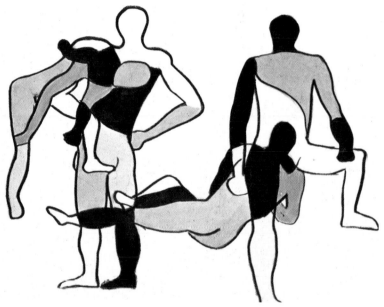

The strong gesture of the figure on the right converging on the figures to the left, echo color and pattern. This is a forceful spatial arrangement.

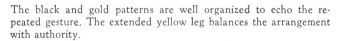

The black and gold patterns are well organized to echo the repeated gesture. The extended yellow leg balances the arrangement with authority.

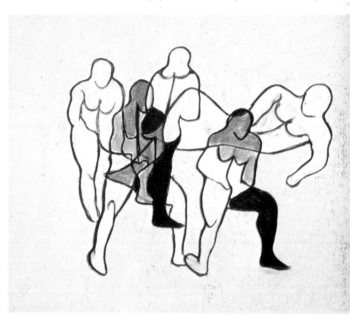

A stronger use of overlap shapes could improve this composition.

This three-figure arrangement does not contribute to the unity of the gesture drawings. Spatially it's rather pleasant.

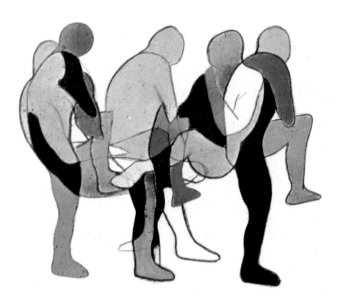

This repeated gesture is done with style and taste. The black shapes unify the composition.

Cerulean blue, pale yellow, and black were used with considerable inventiveness. This is a well organized composition.

FISHERMAN, Oil
collection Leonard Starr, New York

56

The Monotype
or Monoprint

Maurice Prendergast

FOR MANY YEARS the Monotype has been a much neglected medium, notwithstanding the fact that such great artists as Rembrandt, Leonardo da Vinci, Degas and Paul Klee, and many others used the medium. My purpose in introducing you to the Monotype techniques is to show you a variety of possibilities in experimenting with form, line, mass, textures and tonal qualities of great variety. Because the print is the reverse image of the drawing done on the inked glass, the result will often have a surprising visual impact not anticipated in the drawing.

The Monotype is an off-set transfer technique produced directly from any polished surface — preferably glass, or smoothly polished metal.

Prints can be made with oil color, printer's ink, or water soluble block printing ink. In our school workshop we used water soluble ink for several reasons. It is cheaper than oil color or oil-based printing inks. It is fast drying, and because it is water based it is easier to clean up after a studio session. Also, its fast drying qualities permit over-printing of color and line.

I recommend three different methods of Monotype printing. The first is called the direct method. In this method the image is painted directly on the glass plate, either with a brush, a palette knife, or by squeezing color on the plate directly from the tube.

The image produced by applying the color in this manner is then transferred to paper, resulting in an off-set print. This medium affords many possibilities for rapid expression in color mood, mass, and linear patterns. It allows the artist to explore visual ideas at little cost in time and money. The experience gained here can become a valuable rehearsal for painting in oils, water color or acrylics.

I call the second method the indirect. Here the plate is first inked with a solid layer of pigment. This is either rolled on or brushed on with a stiff bristle brush to give you either a smooth line and tone or a textured line and tone. Draw the shapes and images by placing printing paper over the inked plate and then sketch on the paper with a lead pencil. You can render several thicknesses of line by using varied pencils, the back of a brush or a piece of wood. Degrees of recessiveness or frontality can be achieved by exerting differing pressures on the pencils. A great variety of textures can be produced and accidental effects can be exploited to create provocative effects.

Number three is the hard-edge method. I devised this way of printing to help my students to enlarge their experience with shapes and color patterns. The present popularity of hard-edge painting has created a great deal of interest among students. This is a fast and economical way to achieve interesting results in this area. Start this printing process by rolling a generous amount of color over the entire plate to ensure an even printing quality. After you've established the color, the plate is ready for drawing. Use a single edged razor blade flatly to scrape or cut out around the important areas to develop shapes and patterns. If you dry each color properly you can overprint many with dramatic results.

COLOR

Before we go into the explanation of procedure in monotype printing, I want to discuss the many ways in which you will be using color. We will not be concerned with theory but rather with a practical and workable way to use the recommended colors.

By limiting your palette you will be forced to use these colors with ingenuity and invention. You will have constructive fun. I've recommended six colors in this palette. Red, yellow, and blue are the bright primary hues; brown, black, and white are mixing colors from which you will be making grays, tints, tones and monochromatic harmonies.

Let's start with the three primary colors: red, yellow and blue.

From these three primary colors you can mix secondaries that are a mixture of two primary colors. For example: orange is a mixture of red and yellow, green is a mixture of yellow and blue, and violet is a mixture of blue and red. We can go on to further mixing of primary and secondary colors to make intermediary colors. Scarlet is a mixture of red and orange. To get yellow-orange mix orange and yellow. Chartreuse is a mixture of yellow and green. For turquoise mix green and blue. Blue-violet is a mixture of blue and violet and for purple mix violet and red.

The manufacturers of the colors we're using — block printing inks — do not label their colors as the makers of standard oil and watercolor do. For example: reds are called cadmium red, light, medium, and deep; yellows are called cadmium yellow, light, medium and deep; blues are called ultramarine, light, deep, cobalt, and manganese or cerulean blue. There are many earth colors available in oils and watercolors which are not available in block printing colors. These colors are called burnt sienna, burnt umber, raw umber, raw sienna, yellow ochre, light and deep, and mars yellow. You can, however, approximate most of these colors by adding three colors to your palette, namely, brown, black, and white.

The following basic color mixtures can be made from your three primary colors and the addition of brown and black. Make yellow ochre from yellow plus a little brown; the more brown you use the darker the yellow ochre. For burnt sienna use yellow plus red and a little brown. For burnt umber use red and brown in equal mixture. Mix raw umber from red, yellow, and black in almost equal proportions. To get cold gray, mix white and black in any proportion depending on the value you wish to attain. For warm gray, white, black and a touch of yellow will make a driftwood gray. If you want it a little warmer add a touch of brown. There are many tints and tones to be made from your recommended colors and again I advise you to consult the Color Key color wheel for further study.

2. I've painted into the dabs of red with my palette knife. By spreading the color around casually I found that I had developed an interesting abstract shape. I have also developed an echo of this same color.

3. Before this shot was taken I had squeezed out yellow and some brown. Mixing the two I was able to make yellow ochre. I mixed some white with my yellow to make it more opaque.

1. Here I'm mixing white into a dab of red to make a pink. Now we have orange, red and pink showing on the plate.

4. After squeezing out some blue, I decided that it was too dark and I lightened it with white. Because such decisions are often made intuitively, it's hard to explain why you make them.

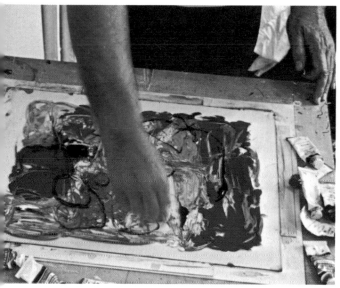

5. I'm drawing passages by squeezing the color out of the tube. The accidental effects often obtained in this way can form a rhythmic movement.

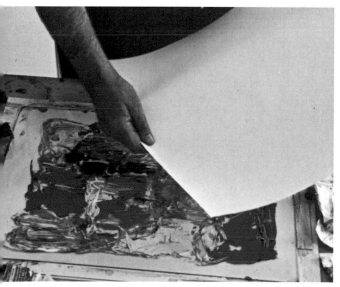

6. After some minor adjustments in color I decided to print the result. Notice how I am holding the print paper. Practice placing the paper on the plate for a black and white in a dry run.

MATERIALS

GLASS-PLATE, cut to 14″ by 17″ from single weight window glass. Grind the sharp edges to a smooth roundness or have a glazier do it. You can do this with a file, a carborundum stone, or a piece of sandpaper. This eliminates the chance of cutting your hand while handling the plate.

PRINTING INKS — I recommend water soluble block printing inks. Although I dislike plugging any manufacturer's goods, I will recommend any product I've found to be superior. In this case Grumbacher block printing inks proved to be very acceptable. These inks are brilliant and mix very well. I like their consistency and right drying qualities. I would like you to limit your palette to three primary colors: red, yellow, and blue in addition to brown, black, and white to make a total palette of six colors.

Also one or two 4 inch sprayers or rollers.

A palette knife 4 to 6 inches long preferably with a stiff blade.

A painting knife with a 4 inch long flexible blade.

Illustration board, mat board or mount board, 20 by 30 inches. From this cut four strips 1 by 10 inches to use for cradling the glass plate.

One box of single edge razor blades. Buy industrial-size package at a hardware store. The package holds 100 blades and they're cheaper this way.

One small bottle of Elmer's glue for cementing down the strips.

A viscose kitchen sponge cut in two.

Two or three coffee or tomato cans for water.

A disposable paper palette 11 by 14 inches for mixing special colors.

Four drawing lead pencils HB - 3B - 4B - 6B.

A drawing board or a piece of half-inch plywood 22 by 30 inches.

A box of thumb tacks and one box of metal push pins with half inch points.

One Gainsborough pig bristle brush No. 14 - One No. 12 - One No. 8 and one No. 6.

Have plenty of clean rags. Old sheets and pillow cases are best.

Use a bond paper pad of 16 pound layout paper. The sizes are 18 by 24 inches or 19 by 24 inches depending on manufacturer.

One 17 by 24 inch pad of newsprint paper.

Have plenty of daily newspapers around for blotting while you are in the process of printing.

The final procedure on this print is the blotting to absorb all the excess ink. Make your first blotting with a sheet of bond paper. You can often make another offset print this way. Follow up by blotting with newspaper until you are satisfied that the print is fully absorbed. Allow 24 hours drying time before you file the print away. If the image left on the plate is still tacky, try for another print. If this second effort comes up thin and pale keep it for further development by overprinting. If you are lucky you may get two or three prints which could be used as the basis for overprinting.

You can use the color left on the plate for another interesting experiment. Remember that the ink is water-soluble and therefore still usable.

Saturate the viscose sponge with water. With this wet sponge, dab — don't rub — the color left on the plate until it is completely saturated. Some of the colors will begin to blend into one another and produce some very fluid effects. Make sure that all the color is dissolved before you start printing. If there are areas that contain too much water, a puddle, squeeze out the sponge and take up these areas. Try to do this without disturbing the image.

Print up this fluid color-image by very gently placing the paper on the plate to avoid smudging. Start printing with the palm of your hand, again, with very little pressure at first. Allow the paper time to absorb the very wet spots. Peel back the print to see what you are developing. You may be pleasantly surprised. Whatever the results, this fluidly abstract print will be useful to you later. Blot and dry the print and store it for further development. Follow this same procedure each time you make a direct color print. After a short while you'll not only have a collection of prints of direct effort, but you'll have many second and third prints which will be useful to you later.

Some of my students dry their prints by hanging them on clips. Don't stack prints until you have blotted thoroughly.

The spontaneous effects you can create with water will suggest ideas for overprinting. Many artists wet their paper to produce soft-textured effects in monoprinting. I don't recommend bond paper for this if you use water-soluble ink. Bond paper wrinkles very badly after it is dried, making it useless for further development in overprinting. Artists who use oil color or printers ink with turpentine or mineral spirits as a medium find any paper useful. Such prints dry absolutely flat. If you care to experiment with oil mediums you may follow the same recommended procedures, with one added precaution. The oil or printer's ink and turpentine prints need much more drying time, at least 24 hours before you can overprint or file them.

After you've had experience in monotype printing and wish to expand to a more professional level, you might like to invest in a better quality of printing paper. One of the best, and that which is used by many professional artists, is Japanese rice paper. I use a rice paper called SHOGUN. This high quality and beautiful paper comes in sheets 17½ by 22 inches and it has a deckle-edge. By deckle-edge I mean the unfinished, rough edge of handmade paper. Many artists frame their prints to show this deckle-edge. It is the mark of handmade craftsmanship. This paper can be purchased in light and heavy weights.

After placing the print carefully on the plate, I printed up the results. Using the palm of my hand, I applied a light and even pressure all over the back of the print. I stress light pressure because a sudden heavy pressure does not give the paper time to absorb the excess ink, thereby forcing the colors to squish into one another. After you have applied four or five passes with your hand, peel back the print as shown in the photograph. Once again I repeat the caution, peel back the print very slowly. If the offset of color is as rich and luminous as the original painting on the glass, then the print is a success.

1. After squeezing ink over the plate, I brush over the surface. Do not brush up to the edge of the glass. My purpose is to print only the line from the center part of the plate.

2. Here my hand is brushing the ink back and forth in many directions, applying the color in a cross-hatch way. The stiff pig bristles of the No. 14 brush produce the texture that we want for the etching-like line.

3. I am blotting the plate to absorb all excess ink and to help dry it enough to ensure good printing quality of line. If the ink is too soupy the paper will be attracted to it by its own weight and ruin your chances for clarity and crispness. A certain amount of accidentally textured tonal quality is good, but it is a matter of degree. After blotting the plate, pass your brush over the surface again in the same cross-hatch manner. Allow about two to four minutes for the ink to set up before placing the paper over the plate.

4. Notice how the index finger and thumb of my left hand are holding the print down. I'm using an HB drawing lead pencil sharpened to a good point. These lines should be intuitive rather than deliberate and studied. Until you become adept at figure drawing, try simpler things.

5. The finished print. Note the fluid linear work without conventional proportion or detail. This should be the approach when working in this technique.

INDIRECT LINEAR PRINTING METHOD

This next section is illustrated with progressive photographs in black and white. This is a class demonstration and it shows, step-by-step, how to make a brushed-on linear print. The quality of line produced by this brushed-on method has the visual impact of an etching or engraving. It contains many surprises in frontality and texture. I recommend this technique for developing pictorial ideas and imposing imagery over tonal color tints, tones, or chromatic color harmonies. The effects produced in this way can be as rich as prints produced by lithography, intaglio or etching. Naturally the great advantage in all graphic mediums is the benefit of the multiple print.

1

2

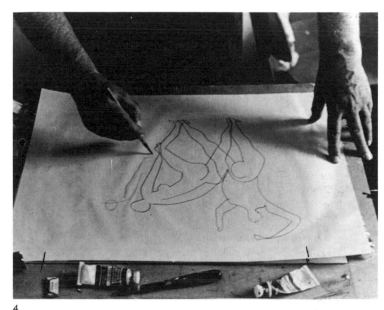

4

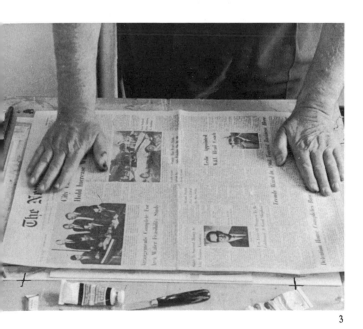

3

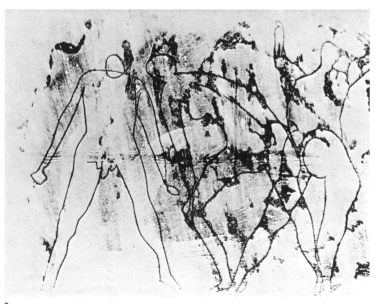

5

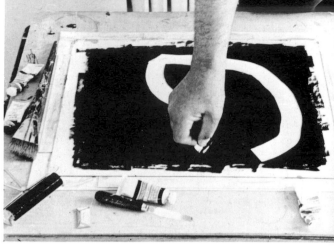

HARD-EDGE DIRECT PRINTING

MANY OF MY STUDENTS were interested in the current popularity of hard edge painting, so I devised this printing method to give them some experience in this area. This demonstration was done with black ink. However, that does not mean that you are limited to the use of black. Beautiful hard edge prints can be made with multiple color printing. Many harmonious colors can be rolled on the plate at one time. Scraping into these colorful patterns can be a very exciting experience. The color patterns themselves can motivate the discovery of provocative shapes.

3 This shows my hand cutting into the inked surface to draw a free-form shape. Make your shapes simple, but dramatic.

1 Ink is being squeezed out of the tube and distributed over the plate in a small quantity of about an inch long.

4 I am executing a tricky move because I got some ink on my thumb and didn't want to mess up the print. The proper way to hold the print is with the thumb and index finger.

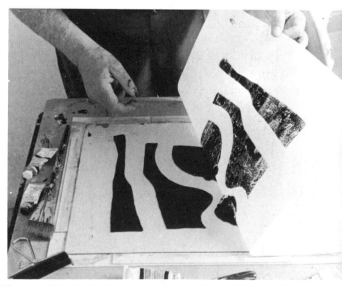

2 The inking is almost complete. You can usually tell by the "feel" of the ink if you have an even distribution. In the next procedure you will be using single edged razor blades to scrape color. Each scraping requires the use of a new blade because they develop nicks which show up as black lines in the negative areas.

5 I am peeling back the print to inspect the printing results so far. I caution you to peel slowly. The result of the inspection proved that a few areas needed more printing. I proceeded by applying more pressure with my hand and finally using the brayer in a few areas. A slight touch of brown in a pool of yellow will give you a very acceptable yellow ochre.

62

Critique of Student Monotype Prints

Here's a suggestion to students. File your prints after they are thoroughly dry, by placing a piece of clean newsprint paper from your 18 by 24 inch pad between them. These prints will be useful to you later when you start to paint in oil or acrylic. Many of the visual ideas developed in the monotype medium can be a rehearsal for painting. Many of my students wanted to work in graphics mediums such as lithography, etching intaglio, and silk screen printing. Graphics are naturally more acceptable as fine arts media. The various methods of printing require professional know-how and expensive equipment. Many universities have very fine departments in graphics. There are many first-rate printers who will process an edition for you for a reasonable fee. The great advantage of working with graphic mediums is the multiple print. Interest in graphic mediums has been growing tremendously in the past few years. New and exciting printing techniques and large scale colorful prints are very much in demand by collectors all over the world.

This was done by dripping and squeezing color out of a tube. The drawing shows considerable control in a very "chancey" way to work.

This is an action painting done in red and black on white paper by the direct method. Both colors were painted on the plate with the brayer, resulting in some spontaneously accidental gestures that recall the work of Franz Kline. It took one printing.

Here's an abstract fantasy produced by two direct method printings. The first impression was done by manipulating the brayer over some small patches of cool and warm color. This was dried. The polly-wog like images were dripped on the plate right out of a tube of black ink. Here and there the artist dabbed small areas with the neck of the tube. The accidental effects, as well as the controlled, are very valid. ➡

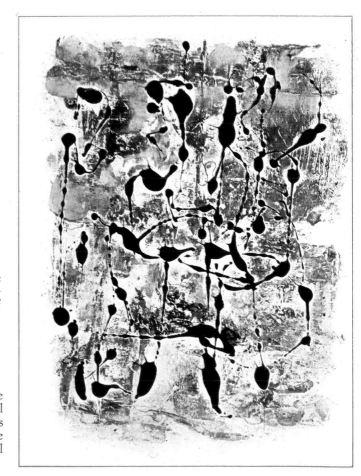

1. An amusing print of faces and things with surrealist overtones. The textured linear work was done over a second or third printing from a direct method print. A direct and indirect method print. Two printings.

2. What seems at first to be a landscape with clouds overhead, at closer inspection reveals loosely drawn figures. The color is blue, darkened with a little black to make a blue-black.

3. This abstract landscape was done by rolling on deep blue, blue green, and yellow ochre. A direct method of printing.

4. This is a religious theme. The artist used hard-edge and indirect methods; the free form shapes were cut into an inked plate of brown. The color was mixed with brown, yellow and white; the result was a dark ochre. A print was made, blotted, dried and registered to provide a guide for overprinting. The good register here is important.

5. This is rendered by two printings in the direct method. The red was painted and printed first. The corners of the print were registered by the recommended method. The red image was then blotted with newspaper until everything but a faint unprintable image remained. This light veil then became the guide for the painting of the black symbol.

6. Here's an abstract image in two colors, dark blue and dark green. This was done as a demonstration of the hard-edge method of printing by the author. The shapes were incised with a single edge razor blade. It took one printing.

7. On top of this abstract print, the student imposed a representational drawing of two women. Since the drawing was done freely, the result is loose and imaginative. The drawing was photographed from the reverse side of the finished print.

4

5

6

7

Student Critique all media

Acrylic polymer color was used for this painting. It's 38 x 50 inches. It was painted on acrylic primed cotton duck canvas which had been primed with a deep warm gray ground. The motivation for this painting comes from the student's interest in architectural forms, and from his study of space concepts. True perspective was ignored here; each segment of the whole module having its own vanishing point. The "see through" shapes contribute immeasurably to the depth perception. This painting won a purchase award at the University, and it well deserved the honor.

Acrylic polymer color on gesso primed linen canvas, size 40 x 50. Motivated by a color photograph of an Italian Agonda automobile grid, this is a hard-edge painting of excellent taste and quality.

Oil painting on canvas, size 40 x 50. The painting was done in the alla prima from several newspaper photographs of DeGaulle.

Acrylic on gesso canvas, size 40 x 50. Motivated by the view from the studio window, this is very impressive translation of realism into today's hard-edge consciousness. The painting reflects the artist's well ordered talent.

Acrylic on canvas, size 40 x 50. The motivation was just an urge to paint with bright color. This may be the reason why this painting started as something entirely different in concept.

Acrylic polymer color on cotton canvas with gesso ground. Interpreted from published copy and motivated by a strong interest in color and pattern. There is a Charles Sheeler quality in this painting with strong black patterns dominating the structure of the composition. This student won a University purchase prize with this painting in 1967.

Acrylic polymer on a gesso-primed cotton canvas. Size 40 x 46 inches. Motivation, a photograph of a street traffic light advertising a product. This artist carefully selected the important aspects of this image to translate to a painting a common image and give it the dignity of a museum piece.

Acrylic polymer on acrylic primed cotton canvas, size 20 x 30. Motivated by the student's interest in racing cars. Source of material was a small color snapshot taken during a race at the Indianapolis 500. Here the field of flat color areas are well balanced allowing the free form of the red seat cover to dominate.

Acrylic polymer on a gesso-primed cotton canvas, size 40 x 50. Student has interest in sociology. The source of material was a well publicized piece of photographic copy on race relations. Although a bit too graphically translated, it nevertheless has considerable personal implication. The figures were painted on a buff-colored ground with acrylic color. The linear contours were drawn with pressed charcoal after the flat color areas were painted in. The composition could be less linear and survive.

Acrylic polymer color on gesso primed cotton canvas, size 20 x 30. This student's motivation comes from a strong desire to express inner emotions with imaginative concepts. You sense this young man's subject matter but you find more interest in his color and fluent line.

Acrylic polymer color on gesso primed cotton canvas. Size 30 x 40 inches. The motivation stems from the student's interest in old wood burning locomotives. The source of the pictorial material was an old engraving print of a locomotive named "Troy". The engraving was in black and white, which permitted the artist to supply color of his own choice. In interpreting the drawing of the print he allowed himself some license in changing proportions and details. Painting was done on a pure white ground of gesso. A careful drawing in vine charcoal was developed in full detail. He proceeded to paint the largest areas of color first, cautiously enlarging the work to contain the details.

Oil painting on oil primed canvas. Size 24 x 32 inches. Painted in the direct method from careful drawings made from detailed photographs of an American coal-burning locomotive, motivation was the student's interest in machinery design. The title is appropriately "The Great American Wheel". This is a fine example of interpretation from published copy, done with restraint and respect for spatial values.

Mixed media painting, 40 x 50. Acrylic polymer, charcoal and pastel were used with considerable professional flair. Motivation was created by the student's interest in sociology. The source of material for subject was selected from published copy and skillfully translated.

Oil painting on primed linen canvas, size 36 x 44. Motivation was the student's interest in old Virginia buildings and landscape. He made many trips on his motorcycle to record his impression of this site. He paints on a tinted ground prepared with turpentine and raw umber. He starts his paintings with slashes of bright color which are later toned down with veils of high key opaque color. This technique explains the reason for the broken-color quality in this painting.

Oil painting on acrylic primed canvas, 30 x 42 inches. It was painted in the alla prima technique with predominantly impasto color. It was motivated by abstract expressionist ideas and from experience obtained in monotype printing. Color and shape in geometric fractions combine to express a strong image. Warm and cool colors are well orchestrated. A good painting by a dedicated student.

Oil painting on gesso-printed cotton canvas. Size 22 x 36. Motivated by interest in Charles Sheeler's highly simplified realism, the technique employed was direct painting in built-up layers of lean oil color over a lightly tinted ground. A careful drawing was first made of a basin and a pitcher. The painting has considerable design impact.

Acrylic polymer on gesso primed masonite, size 22 x 34. Motivation comes from this student's preoccupation with subtleties of textures, tonal qualities, and lyrical landscape. He follows the same representational path as Andrew Wyeth, whom he greatly admires. There is a *trompe-l'oeil* quality in much of his work and it is prominently visible in the way he painted the wire fence and the oil lamp. There is a serenity and calm about this picture which must in some way reflect his satisfaction in communion with nature.

A mixed media collage employing wood and masonite, 30 inches square. The support is made of heavy-grade masonite with glued wood supports on the back to prevent warping. The ground is sprayed white enamel. The three-quarter inch pine wood shapes were "gleaned" from the bottom of the bandsaw at the lumber mill. They can therefore be considered found objects.

Materials & Procedures

ACRYLIC

AT THIS POINT you have had experience in many different mediums. You will naturally want to extend your experience to include working with more sophisticated and mixed media: acrylic, oils, and collage. For this reason I offer you a list of recommended media which can be bought at any art materials' store.

I will start with acrylic polymer plastic paint which has become very popular among students as well as top professionals. The color is flexible and brilliant and highly adhesive. Because it is a water-based color, brushes can be washed easily in tap water. There is very little change in color value from the wet to the dry stage. Acrylics can be used very thinly like water color, or they can be used as impasto. It dries quickly which permits overpainting one color over another without difficulty. All the colors have fine covering qualities. With some practice the color can be used for complete modeled effects (Chiaroscuro), or for flat decorative effects such as is practiced in hard edge painting, pop or op art, and minimal, or shaped canvas.

Pick up a color card at any art materials' store and select an assortment of colors that interests you. The following selection is recommended. These are basic colors and can be mixed to produce great varieties of secondary hues, tints and tones.

Titanium white — large tube (you will use lots of white for mixing) — also mars black, raw umber, burnt umber, yellow ochre light, raw sienna, burnt sienna, ultramarine blue, manganese blue, thalo green, cadmium yellow light, cadmium yellow medium, hansa or cadmium orange, cadmium red light, cadmium red medium, thalo crimson.

Many more colors are available but none that cannot be mixed with this recommended set.

Also include Gesso — a large jar — to be used for priming canvas or boards.

For mixing palette use the glass printing plate recommended for monotype printing. The round water color mixing pans will come in handy later as will all your water color brushes.

A disposable palette 15x18" can be a useful ally. You can put your palette and painting knives to good use with either acrylic or oil painting.

I recommend a variety of tapered nylon brushes. They can be used for both oil and acrylic.

Get sizes 6, 10, 12 and 16.

It is essential that you wash your brushes with soap and water when you are finished. Should you forget and the paint dries on the bristles, do not try to loosen the paint by bending the hairs, this breaks them and ruins the brush. Buy a can of denatured alcohol or laquer thinner and soak the bristles in this chemical until they are good and soft, then wash them with soap and water.

If your color should harden on your glass palette, scrape it off with a sharp new single-edge razor blade. The aluminum water color palettes can be immersed in a bucket of hot water for about 20 minutes to clean them.

Don't forget to have plenty of clean rags handy while you are painting.

There are many commercial painting boards on the market. I recommend stretched acrylic primed canvas to my students. Many art dealers carry canvases already stretched in varied sizes. However, I believe that you should learn to stretch your own canvas. There is a sense of pride and craftsmanship that goes with this first act in your painting.

Many artists who work in acrylic using the alla prima or direct method of painting use an easel. However, large areas of flat color in acrylic are best painted on a flat surface, such as a drawing table or drawing board. The thin consistency of the color precludes working on a vertical surface.

OIL

THE MOST SATISFACTORY MEDIUM to use for oil painting is "gum spirits of turpentine." Gum spirits is the pure turpentine, and it should not be confused with a commercial product called wood turpentine. The cheapest way to buy it is by the gallon.

Turpentine will keep your color wet for many hours, allowing you opportunity to model colors or paint in the "wet into wet" technique. When you desire a much longer drying period use poppyseed oil, a pure slow drying medium that will not change the quality of your colors. For accelerating drying time use Cobalt drier (Linoleate). A very small amount should be used with your color.

Two varnishes are recommended for oil painting. The first is a spray retouch varnish to be used while painting to brighten dull or "sunken in" areas of color; this will also help you to compare the values or the chroma of your colors by rendering the dried-in areas to look wet again. After your canvas is thoroughly dry, spray it very lightly with Damar varnish. If a second spray is required, spray only the areas that have gone matte.

Most oil paintings are done on easels; however, this is not

absolutely necessary. I know many professionals who don't use them; they hang stretched canvas from two nails set into a wall. The prices of easels run from about $6.50 to $100.

MIXED MEDIA — OIL AND ACRYLIC

FROM PETER BRUEGHEL AND JAN VAN EYCK to many 19th and 20th century painters the underpainting technique has been widely used. Many of the Old Masters including the early Flemish painters used tempera as an underpainting medium. Underpainting is an extension of the design or drawing and it usually establishes the flat tonal values of the subject matter in monochromatic color. Brighter transparent glazes of color are imposed over the underpainting to develop the forms. This has been the most widely used mixed media technique in the history of painting.

Degas, Manet, Monet, Bertha Morisot and many contemporary Europeans and Americans used varied mixed media techniques in painting. Pastel, charcoal, ink, water color acrylic has all been used effectively as underpainting media for over painting in oils.

The alla prima technique is a method of direct painting by a single application of pigments used either fat or lean. The entire image is realized with direct and positive brush strokes. The glib and masterfully brushed portraits of John Singer Sargent are impressive examples of direct painting.

COLLAGE

COLLAGE IS A TECHNIQUE developed from the early experiments of Pablo Picasso, Braque and other innovators of the time, to the high sophistication of the surrealist painter such as Max Ernst and collagists Robert Motherwell, Corrado Marca Relli and Esteban Vicente. Such elements as colored papers, newsprint, railway tickets, stencilled letters, lithographed posters, photographs, string, hair, printed and textured fabric, tin foil, aluminum, brass, wire, glass eyes, mirrors, wood, coffee grounds, sand, gravel and many other materials are used. The whole idea comes from a creative urge to relate disparate fragments of a variety of materials, thus provoking shock and interest.

The most important ingredients in collage are a fertile imagination, a lot of curiosity, a pair of scissors, and a good glue, preferably Elmer's. Adequate support is recommended when heavy materials are used; however, a canvas or illustration board can support most flat materials. Mixed media technique is often employed in collage very effectively. Combining acrylic painting with collage is the most commonly used.

One artist I know goes to a great deal of trouble to make a very special binder out of powdered Lucite, which can only be bought in 50 pound containers. When dissolved in a solvent called Toluol it produces a liquid lucite-44. This is a binder as well as a varnish of a high quality transparency. You can buy a gloss medium varnish from any acrylic color manufacturer that can also be used as a binder as well as a varnish. Several good acrylic modeling pastes can be bought also, which can be used for heavy textured effects. Bas-relief or sculpture in low relief, can be attained with this medium.

IMPASTO

IMPASTO PAINTING can be done with either oil or acrylic color. With oil colors underpainting white as well as Titanium white are combined with colors and applied to the canvas without the use of thinning mediums, such as linseed oil, or turpentine. Acrylic colors are pre-mixed with modeling paste extender to give them a heavier viscosity. Impasto painting is usually applied with a palette or painting knife. Vincent Van Gogh, Maurice De Vlaminck, Nicolas De Stael were superb masters of this technique.

GROUND

GROUND IS A COLOR SURFACE applied to the canvas upon which a picture is painted in contrasting colors. Color grounds can be effectively used as a means of unifying colors. Many painters use deep, cool color grounds to paint warm colored pictures, and warm color grounds to paint cool pictures. Deep color grounds will dramatize color and compel you to adjust color to accept the environment. The glazing of a lighter color of thin pigment over a ground can produce transparent colors that can be dramatically expressive.

How To Stretch a Canvas

1. Showing 2 squares of cardboard, tack hammer, canvas pliers, canvas, ruler, and stretcher strips.

THE ESSENTIAL TOOL is a pair of heavy duty canvas-pliers. They have non-slip grips on the jaws. One tack hammer and a supply of no. 3 carpet tacks or a stapling gun with ½ inch staples are also necessary.

The cheapest way to buy your canvas is by the roll. Buy heavy grade cotton duck acrylic, primed. It is less expensive than linen and just as satisfactory to work on.

Start with a small stretcher, 16 x 20 inches. You can work up to larger sizes after you have gained experience. Stretcher strips come in all sizes up to 60 inches. They are pre-fabricated with machine cut corner mitres, tongue and grooved to assure tight corners. They usually come with keys (wedges) which, when hammered into the grooved corners, will take up the slack and tighten the canvas. I prefer not to use these wedges because they tend to throw the stretcher out of square. To assure perfect stretch I recommend cardboard corner pieces made of mat or illustration board. You can make these corner pieces by cutting two squares of stiff cardboard into 5 inch square pieces. Now, cut diagonally across these squares to make four tri-angular corners. Tack or staple these angles to each corner of the stretcher, up to the recessed lip ¼ inch from the outer edge of the stretcher wood. Place the angles up to this lip and tack or staple down securely. For extra large canvases over 40 inches, plywood corners are recommended. One quarter inch or three-eighths plywood is best. These should be *screwed* into the stretcher. These triangular corners will keep your stretcher square at all times, especially while you are hammering or stapling.

2. First two stretcher strips are assembled.

Now, place your canvas on a flat table with the primed side down. Place the stretcher on top of the canvas with the cardboard corner on top side. With a yard-stick or ruler measure one and one-half inches from the edge of the stretcher and draw a straight line, marking the canvas all around. Cut the canvas on this measured line with a pair of scissors. You are now ready to tack or staple the canvas to the stretcher strips.

Because this is tricky business I suggest that you follow the sequence photos and captions for the remainder of the procedure.

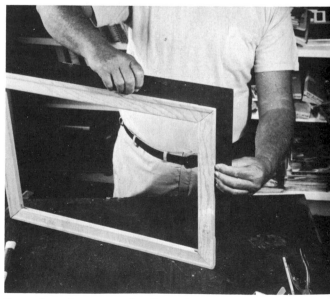

3. Stretcher is squared off with a carpenter's square, or a door frame.

4. Triangular cardboard corners are tacked in place up to the ¼″ lip. Four carpet tacks are used, two on each side of the mitre.

7. Canvas pliers being used properly to get even stretch, always from the center out, alternating even tension everywhere.

5. Canvas is marked 1½″ from the edge all around with a pencil and ruler.

8. The corners are tucked in with a "hospital fold" and secured with one tack.

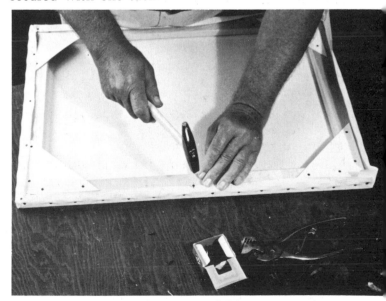

6. Starting the tacking, one tack in the center and one on each side, hammer tacks in half way till finished tacking. Rotate tacking all around adding more tacks each time from each center out to the edge.

9. The surplus canvas showing is folded over and tacked to the back every four inches.

ALLA-PRIMA
Direct painting. The completion of a painting by a single application of pigments, in contrast to a painting which is completed in stages by the application of successive layers of pigments, such as glazing and scumbling over an under-painting.

ARCHAIC
Strictly the styles of antiquity. Also the retention, or imitation of what is ancient, for special purposes.

BROKEN-COLOR
Color which is varied by the introduction of other colors. Strictly speaking, an inevitable condition of painting, since each color is both affected by, and in turn, affects, the colors in proximity.

CALLIGRAPHY
Descriptive of beautiful handwriting; the term has an extended meaning, being applied to the characteristic stroke of an artist's brush or pen.

CHIAROSCURO
The treatment of light and shade in painting. Rembrandt is the great master of chiaroscuro. Earlier the school of Italian chiaroscurists led by Caravaggio (c. 1569-1609) exerted much influence.

COLLAGE
An extension of the technique of Papiers Collès, developed by the Surrealist painter Max Ernst. A collage is a picture or design, composed of such elements as colored papers, newsprint, railway tickets, photographs, engravings, pieces of string, hair, fabric, etc., pasted into a background. The technique was widely employed by the Dadaists as a means of relating disparate fragments of different materials.

COLOR
Glossary of color terms —
HUES are pure bright colors.
TINTS are made by adding white to a hue.
TONES are made by adding black or brown to a hue.

Color *Continued*
VALUE means the lightness or darkness of a color.
CHROMA is the brightness of a color.
MONOCHROMATIC HARMONIES are made by using white, black, or gray with one hue.
HARMONIES OF VALUE can be made by altering the proportions of white, black or gray.

GRAY can also be produced by mixing any two complementary colors. Complementary colors are opposite on the color wheel. For example: blue is opposite to orange — green is opposite to red — yellow is opposite to violet.
Analagous colors are side by side on the color wheel. For example: red is beside orange, yellow is beside green, and blue is beside violet.
You can get all of the above information on color by purchasing the Color Key color wheel mentioned earlier. You can, by dialing the proper colors, find any color you wish. The wheel is beautifully printed in bright colors and you should use it at all times.

CONTOUR
The outline or external boundary of a form. The illusion of of a line enclosing form. An artist may use contour as an element of grace, subtlety, strength, rhythm.

GESSO
Plaster of paris or gypsum. When prepared with a proportion of glue, water etc. gesso provides a ground for wood panels, canvas, preparatory to painting. Or chalk, glue and white.

GLAZE
A transparent, or semi-transparent film of color, applied over a light ground or a lighter color (which must be thoroughly dry).

IMPASTO
A particularly thick or heavy application of paint. It is the contrast of impasted areas with thinly painted passages which often imparts character and robustness to an oil painting, e.g. the thickly painted highlights and thinly painted shadow areas in many of Rembrandt's paintings.

LEAN COLOR
Pigment containing, or used with, a minimum of turpentine or oil.

LOADED BRUSH

A brush which is loaded with pigment ready for the application of a thick, heavy impasto.

MASS

In painting, any large form, or group of forms, or any substantial area of color, light, shade etc. The excellence of composition depends very largely on the skillful organization of mass and space. In composition, mass is considered to be the positive element, and space the negative element.

MIDDLE TONE

In painting, the hue of a tonal value which is half-way between the respective tonal values of light and dark. Sometimes called half-tone, or middle-tone.

MIXED METHOD OR MIXED TECHNIQUE

A method of painting first practiced by early Flemish painters, which consists of completing a tempera underpainting with a series of oil glazes.

SCUMBLE

The reverse of a glaze. A film of opaque pigment applied over a darker color to lighten it.

SYMBOLISM

In art, the expression of an abstract idea in terms of line, form, color, etc. The representation of an object by means of a single, formal equivalent, as in cave art, or the imagery of Byzantine art. In the Freudian sense, Symbolism is extensively employed in Surrealist painting. The use of symbols to imply abstract ideas, e.g. the sexual symbolism employed by Salvador Dali; the medieval symbolistic iconography used by Hieronymous Bosch.

SYMMETRY

Beauty resulting from aesthetic balance. The harmonious organization of subject content; the balancing of one shape, or form, etc., with one similar. The converse of Asymmetry.

TACTILE VALUES

In relation to the work of art, the total experience, both physical and imaginative of apprehending and enjoying a painting; the awareness of distance, space, and mass; of warmth and coolness, stillness and noise, etc. Berenson describes tactile values thus: 'Tactile values occur in representations of solid objects when communicated, not as mere reproductions (no matter how veracious), but in a way that stirs the imagination to feel their bulk, heft their weight, realize their potential resistance, span their distance from us, and encourage us, always imaginatively, to come into close touch with, to grasp, to embrace, or to walk around them.'

TEXTURE

In painting: (a) the representation of the physical characteristics of any particular surface (skin, fabric, wood, metal, earth, etc.); (b) the characteristics of the paint surface itself; whether smooth, rough, etc.

TONE

In the general sense, a term used to describe the 'complexion' of a painting; e.g. 'the golden tone of Venetian painting'; 'the subdued tone of Rembrandt'; the bright tone of Impressionism'. More specifically, a synonym for 'value' used when tonal values of a painting are under discussion or consideration.

TOOTH

The roughness, or grain of the support.

TROMPE L'OEIL

A painting which creates the illusion of actually being what it sets out to depict: e.g. a drop of water on a rose petal, an insect crawling over a flower-stem which looks as though it could be brushed off the canvas. Literally, to deceive the eye. A piece of technical trickery not to be confused with Realism.

VANISHING POINT

In perspective, the point on the horizon line at which parallel lines appear to vanish.

THEY'RE OFF. A group of new students begin at the beginning.

I emphasize the importance of the exercises recommended in the first chapters on geometric form and free form. Acquiring a precise sense of space is vital to the entire course. Follow each chapter progressively, and do not begin the next chapter until you are confident that you have fully explored the contents of the preceding chapter.

It is my sincerest hope that this book will stimulate your interest in drawing and painting, and that the experience will enrich your lives as fifty years of involvement in art have enriched mine.

I feel fortunate in having a family whose interest in this project has been a constant inspiration.
It's a pleasure to dedicate this book to them.
Carolyn, Elena, Tony

— Thank you.